THE STORY OF ARCHITECTURE

**The Marshall Cavendish
Learning System
Editorial Advisory Board**

Marshall Cavendish Books, London WI

Marshall Cavendish Books Limited
58 Old Compton Street, London W1

First published 1969
© Marshall Cavendish Limited 1968
© Marshall Cavendish Books Limited 1969

This book may not be sold in the U.S.A. or Canada
Printed in Great Britain
by Taylor Garnett Evans & Co. Ltd., Watford, Herts.

462 00280 2

Contents

Introduction

Bernard L. Myers
Associate of the Royal College of Art

IT IS still a surprise to some people to learn that the building industry, measured in terms of money invested and labour employed, is the world's biggest industry. All men build, whether a shelter or wind break of a few boughs or a skin tent or thatched hut, an ice hut or a mud hut, or skyscrapers of glass, steel and concrete. Man builds for a variety of purposes; for shelter for himself and his family, for special purposes of work: factories, schools, offices and hospitals, and to the glory of himself or his God: palaces, town halls and parliaments, temples and churches.

Ever since he first started to build he has looked beyond the immediate purpose of the building to something else; to answering a need for both intellectual and emotional satisfaction. It is this additional content of building that goes some way towards a definition of architecture. This quality is not always obvious. It can be lacking in a skyscraper office block and yet found in a South Sea islander's hut or a tribal African village. It does not depend upon size or complex technology; nor upon sculpture, columns and elaborate and expensive decoration. The quality of architecture has often eluded those who most sought after it by trying to copy the great architecture of previous centuries, and yet has appeared in a simple cottage or in a railway bridge when quite unsought after in a conscious way.

Architecture is building reflecting something of the spirit of man. Without this spirit civilization—the art of living in societies—dies. If it is lacking in our towns they become living deserts in which we work and bring up our families very much at odds with our living conditions. It is quite obvious when we look at our average cities, most of which were built during the industrial expansion of the last century, that most of our surroundings have spoilt rather than added something to the world in which we live.

Nowadays the worst of the old towns are

being gradually demolished and new towns are being built. Architecture is no longer a historical study for experts but that art which to a large extent governs the way we live. The question is, what sort of houses, what sort of towns do we wish to live in. To answer this question we must all find out more about the art of architecture and the science of building. This volume, the first of two volumes dealing with architecture yesterday and today, explains what it is we value in the buildings of the past. The second will explain the architecture of today and tomorrow.

Houses of God

Temples of Olympian splendour, soaring Gothic edifices, the functional buildings of modern design – all, whatever their form, reflect men's desire to make monuments to glorify their gods.

IT IS in the Mesopotamian plain between the Tigris and Euphrates rivers that there exists the earliest evidence of religious buildings showing a positive architectural concept. From the fourth-millennium BC temples at Eridu, we find tall buildings with a formal symmetrical layout. The typical temple form was the *ziggurat,* a stepped or ramped pyramid, often rising from a platform itself elevated high above the plain. Mesopotamia generally had little building stone: most buildings were therefore of mud-brick and unfortunately are almost entirely lost to us today.

A dramatic gloom

In contrast, the abundance of stone in Egypt and the vast slave-labour resources have left us a legacy of great monuments dating from the third millennium BC. Stone is, however, limited in the distance it can span a gap as a flat beam between supports. As a result, roofed areas of Egyptian temples are filled with closely spaced rows of columns. In the hypostyle hall the light entered, mainly from windows in the upstanding central part of the roof, producing a dramatic gloom. Such a deliberate restriction of light to induce awe and create an atmosphere of devotion and reverence recurs throughout the history of religious architecture.

In the Egyptian temple, however, this psychological effect was reserved for the king and his priests, for, unlike the congregational buildings of Christianity and Islam, these temples were not places for public worship: they were sacred enclosures for the performance of secret ritual.

Nor was the Greek temple a congregational building, but it was much more a part of public life. The Greeks were great colonizers, and founded settlements from Asia Minor to Sicily, some of which (like Agrigento in Sicily and Paestum in Campania) today possess more complete remains of Greek Doric temples than many city sites in Greece itself.

The Greek temple consisted basically of a *cella,* a divided walled chamber, surrounded by a colonnade, the whole being covered with a pitched roof forming triangular pediments at each end. These and the friezes on both the inside and

The best preserved of the few Doric temples remaining in Greece itself, the Theseion stands on a hill in what used to be the *agora,* or market place, of ancient Athens.

outer walls were filled with sculpture. The Parthenon at Athens, with its subtle refinements, is regarded as the supreme example of Doric architecture: it dates from the time of Pericles, about 440 BC. The Doric order, with sturdy fluted columns with no base, and an undecorated capital, was established by the sixth century BC, and the majority of Greek temples were of this type. The Ionic order originated later in Asia Minor: it is more delicate and ornate than Doric; the slender columns have moulded bases and a complex capital with *volutes* or spirals with egg-and-dart moulding between (the Erechtheion at Athens and the Temple of Artemis at Ephesus are good examples). A third order, Corinthian, was a development of Ionic, having a formalized acanthus-leaf capital (the Olympeion at Athens).

Medieval churches

The Romans inherited the *trabeated* system of flat beams spanning between columns or walls from the Greeks, but they also adopted the arch from the Etruscans, developing it into vault and dome forms (collectively called *arcuated* construction). It is to the Romans' daring experiments with arcuated forms that we owe much of the structural splendour of medieval buildings. They extended arches to form *barrel vaults* (like tunnels) and by intersecting these at right angles formed *cross vaults*. A row of these needs only supporting columns at the corners of each vault; this construction, used in their public baths and basilicas, was the basis of all medieval church structures.

The Romans also experimented with spherical forms, and developed domes of large size. They invented concrete, and exploited its advantages of structural continuity and fluidity to produce great monolithic domes and complex curved shapes. The dome of the Pantheon (built in 124 A D) still stands today; its diameter of 142 feet is greater than that of Michelangelo's dome of St Peter. Most of their temples, however, were rectangular trabeated buildings, the larger ones closely resembling the Greek prototype. The smaller temples (like the Temple of Fortuna Virilis at Rome and the Maison Carrée at Nîmes) usually had only a cella

The roof of the enormous *hypostyle hall* of the Great Temple of Ammon at Karnak, Thebes is supported by 134 columns in 16 rows, for stone beams cannot span any great distance.

S. Giovanni in Laterano, Rome, was one of the great basilican churches founded by the Christian Roman Emperor Constantine. All except the east end has been rebuilt in the Baroque style.

and portico. They stood in the forum with other public buildings, including the basilica. This was a long rectangular building, with rows of columns forming a central space and side aisles, and a semi-circular projection centrally at each end.

The Emperor Constantine officially established Christianity in 313 A D, and initiated a programme of church building which continues to this day. The first churches were of basilica form, as this was suitable for large assemblies, with a focal point at one end, and the existing basilicas

7

S. Maria Maggiore, Rome, built by Pope Sixtus III in 432 is one of the most typical of basilican churches.

could readily be converted. Constantine founded three of the great basilicas of Rome: S. Pietro (330), S. Giovanni in Laterano (330) and S. Paolo fuori le mura (380).

Not all early churches were basilican, however. The Romans' interest in geometry and arcuated forms produced several circular or polygonal churches: S. Stefano Rotondo (470) is an enormous circular church 210 feet in diameter. The Minerva Medica (266) was a ten-sided building with an 80-foot dome; it used for the first time the *pendentive,* a spherical triangle which transmits the load from a circular dome on to a many-sided base, and was the model for similar Byzantine churches centuries later, such as S. Vitale at Ravenna.

Byzantine buildings show great preoccupation with plane and spherical geometry; the plans are often many-sided, with complex vaulting and domes on pendentives. The subtle interplay of the curved surfaces is often accentuated by brilliantly coloured mosaics on a golden ground, which gives these occidental buildings a rare oriental quality. The exterior, however, was usually of plain brick, as in the little Tomb of Galla Placidia at Ravenna (540). This building is the earliest surviving example of the Greek cross plan of four approximately-equal arms; the same form on a larger scale was the basis of several major Byzantine churches such as St. Mark at Venice Inside are 46,000 sq. ft of glass mosaics, the cubes of glass so small that some 50 million separate pieces had to be cut, sorted, selected and fixed. The most famous Byzantine building, now Hagia Sophia at Istanbul, was built by Justinian in 536; its interior is a vast open space 250 by 100 feet.

The influence of Islam

Byzantine churches are found all over southern Europe and show a marked

St. Mark's in Venice reflects the art of Byzantium both in its plan (a Greek cross surmounted by domes) and in its lavish decoration. The magnificent glass mosaics inside depict scenes from the Old and the New Testaments.

resemblance in style and mosaic technique, suggesting that travelling groups of artists were responsible. At Monreale in Sicily one can see a Byzantine interior to a Norman church with Islamic features and a Moorish fountain, reminiscent of the Arabic buildings of southern Spain.

This part of Europe is the northern edge of a vast area extending from Toledo to Calcutta which at various times came under the influence of Islam. The actual building style varies, because the Moslem invaders tended to adopt the existing local forms, but applied their characteristic decoration. The oldest existing Moslem building is the Dome of the Rock at Jerusalem (688) on the former pagan/Christian site of the altar of David, Solomon's Temple and the Temple of Jupiter. This dome, set on an octagon, also links the Roman-Byzantine building

form with the Islamic interior decoration. The religious building of Islam is the mosque: in contrast to Egyptian and Greek temples, this is a house for prayer.

Egypt and North Africa have many mosques dating from the seventh to the fifteenth century. In Spain the oldest Moslem building is the Mosque at Cordova (786), second only to that in Mecca in size. Persian mosques have pointed domes, often with brilliant blue-green and polychrome ceramic facing, pointed-arch arcades and the tapering minarets characteristic of this area. In Turkey, the Islamic style dates from the Ottoman Empire in the fourteenth century; the local Byzantine buildings strongly influenced their design, and Hagia Sophia became the model for Turkish mosques.

India has many splendid mosques and tombs, especially of the Moghuls, like the Taj Mahal (1653). It also reflects its mixed religious background in the great variety of other religious monuments, such as the rock-cut temples at Ajanta and Karli (first century AD) dating from the period between the third century BC and 750 AD when Buddhism was the official religion. Chinese rock-cut temples show clear Indian origins; there are several later Buddhist temple buildings, including the characteristic pagoda. India also has a wealth of other temples, especially Hindu and Jain, the latter notable for the rich and grotesque sculpture covering the whole building.

Returning to the West, we can trace the development of church architecture. With the decline of the Roman Empire, buildings in the former Roman provinces assumed a style based on classical Roman architecture, with Byzantine and local influences. This was known as the Romanesque style. Cross vaults were developed into rib-and-panel vaults, with thick ribs at the intersections of planes and light infill panels. The basilican plan was combined with the Greek cross to form the cruciform Latin cross, with long nave and projecting transepts and east end: this was the basis of most church plans for the next few hundred years. Columns were simple cylinders, heavy and closely spaced, with semi-circular arches between.

The semi-circular arch characterizes Romanesque buildings, appearing also in vaults and the heads of windows and doors, which often had concentric bands of geometric carving. The finest Italian examples are in Tuscany, the cathedral groups (cathedral, baptistry, campanile)

The delicately arcaded porch and marble facing on the walls of Pistoia Cathedral are characteristic of much Romanesque architecture in central Italy.

at Pisa, Lucca and Pistoia. Provence has some richly-carved west fronts as at St Gilles at Arles and Ste Madeleine at Vézelay. In northern France a less ornate style evolved, notable for its twin west towers. It was from Normandy that the Romanesque style reached Britain, hence its English name – Norman.

St Lawrence at Bradford-on-Avon is a rare example of the Anglo-Saxon buildings existing at the Norman Conquest, after which Norman churches were built extensively, although Westminster Abbey

Wells Cathedral in Somerset, England was built in the early phase of English Gothic. Although plain and severe in design, the west front (shown here) is heavily carved.

in this style was started a century earlier. Most English cathedrals retain a proportion of their Norman church, especially Ely, Gloucester, Peterborough and Southwell, while Norwich and Durham are still almost entirely Norman. The Gothic style began in northern France in the mid-twelfth century when the cathedrals of Notre Dame in Paris, Bourges and Chartres were begun. These had a rectangular plan with a wide semi-circular east end, unlike the English cathedrals, which followed the Latin cross plan.

Salisbury, Lincoln and Wells cathedrals were largely built during the first phase of English Gothic (Early English) in the thirteenth century. Its character was plain and severe with clustered columns and simple ribbed vaulting, tall lancet windows and little decoration, although the west fronts were richly carved. In the second phase *(Decorated),* during the fourteenth century, windows were widened and divided with elaborate geometric tracery. Vaulting was broken up with many ribs, and the whole character was richer and warmer. Coloured glass came into use. Characteristic of the third phase *(Perpendicular)* is an emphasis on height, with wide and high windows divided by mullions extending the full height. Soaring naves, as at Canterbury, seem to reach towards the sky. Vaulting became more complex, and decorated fan and pendant vaults appeared (King's College Chapel, Cambridge and Henry VII Chapel, Westminster). This period shows a steady progress toward less and less solid walls, the narrow Norman windows increasing until the ultimate stage in the fifteenth century, when the walls were almost entirely window. Elsewhere in Europe, the Gothic style flourished, generally in similar form, Spain developing a particularly flamboyant style.

The Renaissance which began in Florence in the early fifteenth century found architectural expression in the study of

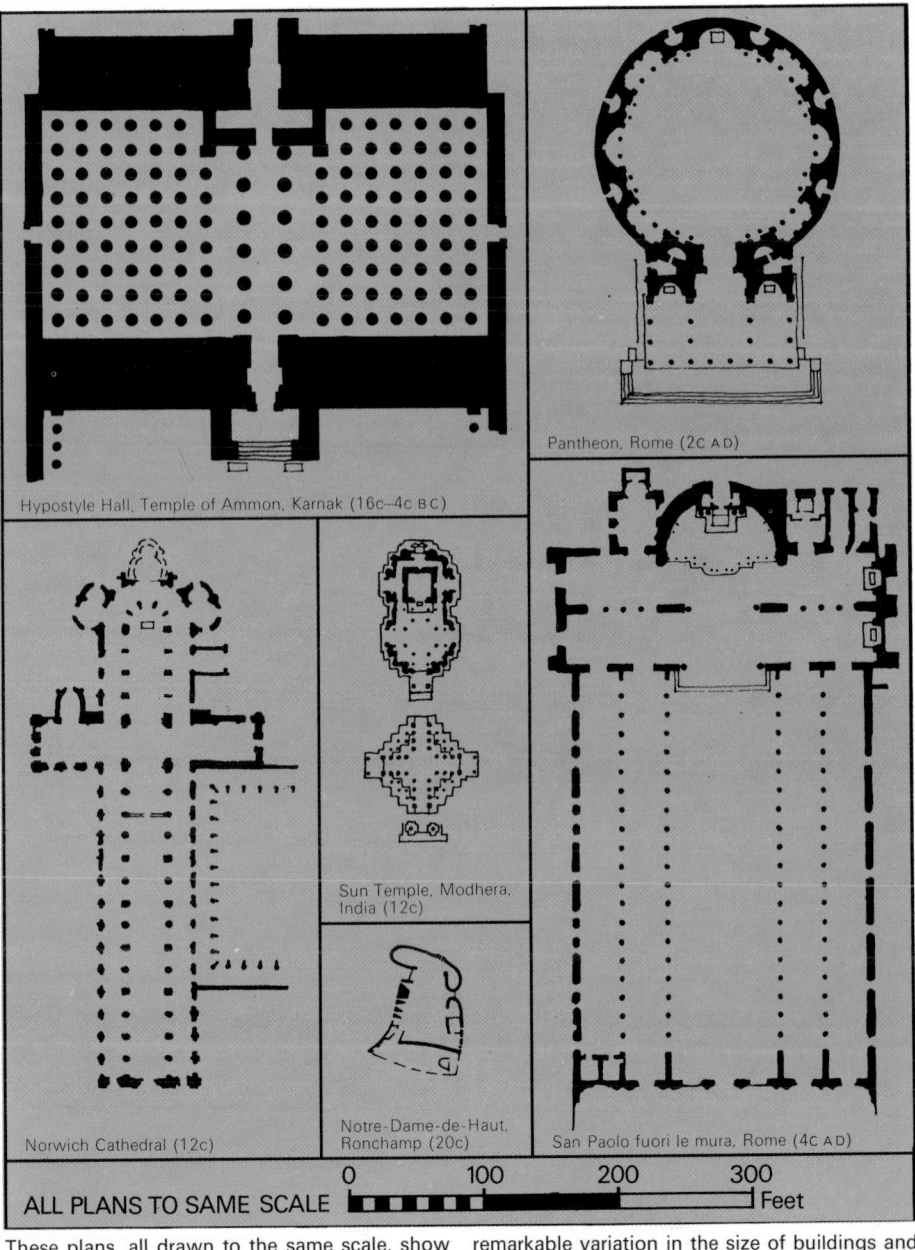

Hypostyle Hall, Temple of Ammon, Karnak (16c–4c B C)

Pantheon, Rome (2c A D)

Norwich Cathedral (12c)

Sun Temple, Modhera, India (12c)

Notre-Dame-de-Haut, Ronchamp (20c)

San Paolo fuori le mura, Rome (4c A D)

ALL PLANS TO SAME SCALE

0   100   200   300 Feet

These plans, all drawn to the same scale, show the development of the plan form and the remarkable variation in the size of buildings and the thickness of walls.

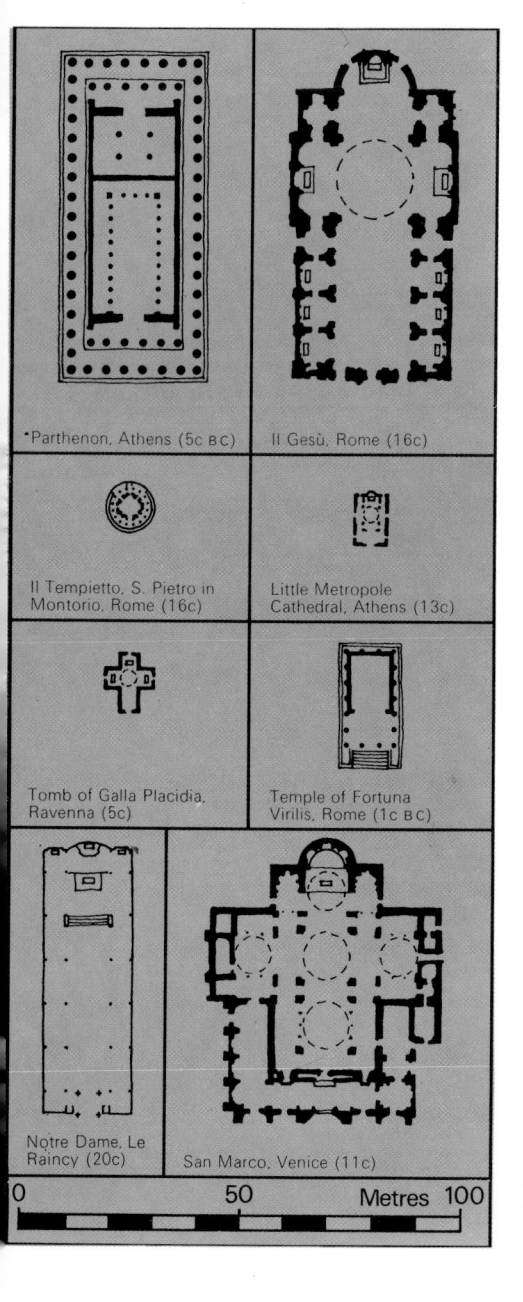

Parthenon, Athens (5c BC)

Il Gesù, Rome (16c)

Il Tempietto, S. Pietro in Montorio, Rome (16c)

Little Metropole Cathedral, Athens (13c)

Tomb of Galla Placidia, Ravenna (5c)

Temple of Fortuna Virilis, Rome (1c BC)

Notre Dame, Le Raincy (20c)

San Marco, Venice (11c)

0   50   Metres 100

Greek and Roman buildings, from which elaborate systems of proportion were evolved. Modified classic columns and entablatures were disposed in regular façades, reflecting the formal symmetrical plans. The Byzantine dome was revived, in a taller form, raised on a colonnaded drum. Lighting was carefully manipulated to dramatic effect, as in Il Gesù, Rome (1575). Bramante's Tempietto (1510) conveys the essence of the style. In the seventeenth century a reaction against the rigid 'prescription' of the Roman architect Vitruvius produced the Baroque, a free and flowing conception, often grand in scale like St Peter's in Rome (1625). The formal style spread to France with the domes of the Invalides (1706) and the Pantheon, Paris (1790), and to England with St Paul's Cathedral, London (1710).

Bogus styles

Among the few churches of the next century, renowned for its domestic architecture, is Nash's All Souls, London (1825). The splendid Victorian engineering achievements were unhappily not paralleled in architecture, where a vogue for the quaint produced an era of revivals of Gothic, and other bogus styles. In France, *Art Nouveau* flourished. One of the few individualists, Gaudí, produced buildings in Spain which at least showed inventiveness. The Church of the Sagrada Familia, Barcelona was begun in 1884 and is still incomplete. The Gothic revival spread to America and in the nineteenth century, reproduction European Gothic churches were built (witness St Patrick's Cathedral and St John the Divine in New York).

More recently, many impressive modern American churches have been built, after the lead in non-derivative design by Le Corbusier in his chapel at Ronchamp, France (1954). In England the major churches designed early in the century (for example Liverpool Anglican Cathe-

Le Corbusier's Chapel of Notre-Dame-de-Haut at Ronchamp, France, exploits the plastic qualities of concrete. Its curving towers and billowing roof contrasts with the rectangular walls.

dral and Guildford Cathedral) clearly display their Gothic origins. Only in the cathedrals at Coventry (1962) and Liverpool Metropolitan (1967) has the problem been faced of designing an ecclesiastical building using the materials and techniques of today honestly and fittingly, while still inducing the emotional response so strongly associated with medieval buildings. Some may find the new forms difficult to accept: a problem which has faced every progressive architect since the time of the Romans.

Houses of Caesar

The gorgeous palaces of by-gone potentates, the huge administrative buildings of our modern world – all are symbols of time and place which outlast the tiny life-span of the age that made them.

MEN, when they have not been erecting shrines to gods, have usually built for their own glory. The history of secular architecture reflects mankind's development as accurately as that of religious architecture. Palaces for both men and governments represent the high-water marks of secular design.

The word *palace* denotes an official residence of a sovereign ruler and derives from the palaces of the Caesars on the Palatine Hill in Rome. Its original meaning became somewhat perverted in the Middle Ages when the term was used to describe the residences of soldier princes and rich merchants. In the Renaissance period the word *palazzo* was employed for the villas and courts of the city-state rulers and eventually became common usage for houses of any powerful family or individual. Its uses today are even more diverse, for it describes any large (usually extravagantly decorated) building, including 'gin palace', 'picture palace' and parliamentary buildings.

During the height of the Roman Empire the world saw an extension of domestic and public building on an unprecedented scale. Rome was rebuilt and every major province had its administrative and residential palace. Together with the earlier Greek examples, the great buildings of Roman times became the standard by which many later powers throughout the world judged their own monuments. Even today, some architects (particularly in the United States) are seeking a revival of classicism in modern dress.

Setting aside for a moment the achievements of the Gothic master builders, it can be argued that the purity and precision of Greek architecture and the power and splendour of Roman building have permeated the whole of Western architectural development. Historians have speculated for centuries why the architecture of antiquity has been such a powerful inspirational force.

Many of the palaces of ancient and classical Greece were situated within the heart of a citadel and often covered acres of land. At Mycenae and Tiryns, strong high walls surrounded the fortresses and access to the heart was restricted. Inside the walls was a large outer courtyard leading into a complex maze of rooms and inner courts. All the important rooms surrounded the minor courtyards. Thus protection from external attack and the encouragement of an internal community life, at least for the rulers and their families, was ensured. The great Cretan palace of King Minos at Knossos, although not fortified like other examples due to its situation, was by all accounts a very civilized place. Sir Arthur Evans's

Almost like a fortified camp, Diocletian's magnificent palace extended along the Adriatic. It once formed the greater part of the medieval town of Spalato (now Split, Yugoslavia).

excavations in 1900 revealed highly sophisticated interiors, plumbing and drainage systems and a royal seat of government that covered 24,000 square yards. Internally the palace was a labyrinth of rooms planned around an enormous central court. Off the main court were the royal apartments, the throne room and the staircases leading to two or three storeys above.

Rome is a palace

With the rise of democracy in later Greek civilization, oligarchy—government by a group—was overthrown. The magnificent buildings used for governmental purposes were no longer the palaces of the autocratic rulers but the new centres of public intercourse and discussion, the *agora* or market places.

The Roman mode of control followed closely the Greek pattern. The first rulers were kings; an intervening period of republican rule was followed by the all-powerful emperors. Rome in the Julio-Claudian age (14–68 A D) was the core of this vast diffused empire. With Nero, the last of the Augustans, many historians concur that a new style emerged incorporating knowledge that had been accumulating over the previous centuries. A major common feature of the new style was the use of vaulted construction.

Nero's Golden House was built after the devastation of the nine days' fire; it was immense, covering much of the Palatine and part of the Esquiline, and beautifully landscaped. The palace was so large in fact that the historian Suetonius records a remark popular in Rome at the time: 'Rome is being made into a palace – off to Veii, citizens, unless Veii too has been taken over.'

Succeeding generations of emperors were to build and extend their palaces on the Palatine and other hills surrounding Rome. It was, however, outside Rome, in

Dalmatia, that one of the last great Roman palaces was built. In 300 AD Diocletian erected his headquarters at Spalato (now Split, Yugoslavia) on the edge of the Adriatic. Here Western and Eastern culture and architecture met. Many principles incorporated in its design lead logically into the Romanesque and Gothic styles.

The palaces of the medieval period were the castles and manor houses of the feudal rulers. They were administration centres for a large area. They were characterized by their fortifications and, up to the fourteenth century, by their spartan interiors. But during that century attitudes were changing and more thought was being given to domestic comfort. In the many examples that remain throughout Europe from that time and later the gradual improvement in living conditions can be seen. The Gothic town house or castle, for example, became a place of display for brilliantly coloured wall hangings, elaborately decorated polychrome timber ceilings and richly carved fireplaces. As the need for fortification grew less, openings became larger and glass and opening windows more common.

In Italy, the great municipal palaces such as the Vecchio and the del Podesta in Florence were modifications of earlier types of fortified castles. The austere Palazzo Vecchio was the seat of government of the Republic and later became the town hall. It proved to be of some importance in the moulding of the early Renaissance style in the city.

The Florentine palaces of the fifteenth century are among the most famous in the world. Initially they derived a certain amount of their decoration and external treatment from the fortified palaces of the previous era. Base storeys were heavily rusticated (faced with masonry cut in massive blocks), with few and small openings. The main living accommodation was to be found on the upper floors and a central

The gracefully arcaded court of the Palazzo Vecchio in Florence belies the severe exterior. Like many medieval palaces, it was a modification of earlier types of fortified castles.

The Palazzo Rucellai in Florence, designed in 1451 by Alberti, broke with early Renaissance design and set the style for buildings of the High Renaissance.

courtyard was usually incorporated. The Palazzo Strozzi (1489) and the Medici-Riccardi (1440–60) are two examples that indicate the stylistic overlap between the medieval and the Renaissance. However, they were built for vastly different motives. No longer was it necessary to build purely for defence and we find that the Strozzi Palace was erected to bring glory and fame to its patron and his family. The Medici-Riccardi was used as both the court and residence of the Medici family. It was later sold to the Riccardi family.

Both of these Florentine palaces are a distinct contrast to the Palazzo Rucellai (1451) by the brilliant architectural theorist Leone Battista Alberti (1402–72). Not only do they look different; they represent a different order. Alberti's town palace was one of the first Renaissance buildings in, which the applied pilaster – a rectangular column – was featured; the Strozzi and the Riccardi were, like many other Florentine palaces of the time, still *astylar* – without columns. It was the revival of this Roman motif by Alberti, together with

his treatise: *De re aedificatoria* (English version: *Ten books of architecture*), completed in 1450, that laid the basis for the buildings of the High Renaissance. Donato Bramante owed much to Alberti but in his buildings the Roman origins of the Renaissance are further exemplified.

Although he was born in Florence, Bramante's best known work is in Rome, where he became the key figure in the development of the High Renaissance. Here he and his distinguished contemporaries designed town houses and villas for the nobility and the princes of the Church. They charged their work with a vitality that remains unsurpassed in the history of architecture. The effects of the High Renaissance were felt throughout the civilized world, but it was in France that it went through its most effective transmutation, producing an individualistic and essentially national style.

Francis I was a prolific builder of palaces. Immediately after his accession in 1515 he rebuilt a wing of the château at Blois in an odd, but beautiful, combination of Gothic and Renaissance details of which included an open spiral staircase topped by a parapet. With the building of the Château of Chambord, Francis created one of the most incredible structures in France, a structure extravagant enough to represent his own greatness. Its formal planning is based on the medieval fortified castle but the well-articulated façades, particularly those of the central block, are clearly Renaissance. The roof to this

Above: The château at Blois, begun in the thirteenth century, is a harmonious mixture of four main styles. Francis I rebuilt one wing in a beautiful combination of Gothic and Renaissance, while the main façade facing the gateway to the court is Baroque.
Below: Francis I loved to build palaces to represent his own greatness. His masterpiece, the Château of Chambord, combines aspects of the fortified castle with Renaissance features.

18

19

central block is unique, sprouting dormers and chimneys in gay abandon.

The king was also responsible for commencing work on two other great palaces, Fontainebleau and the Louvre, the Parisian centre of government. Eventually the Louvre was to have a handsome and gigantic successor: the Palace of Versailles, built for Louis XIV by the architect Le Vau and later extended and transformed by Jules Hardouin-Mansart.

Versailles has been called the world's most sumptuous palace. With its overpowering scale, its magnificent geometrically laid-out park by Le Notre, its inner glory, the lushness of its decor (including the superb Hall of Mirrors by Mansart) and the meticulous care taken in its details, it does indeed typify the seat of Absolute Monarchy, that political firmament from which the Sun King radiated his glory. Architecturally, Versailles represents a turning point in French classicism. Gone were the high roofs of previous châteaux, gone too were the formal axial features breaking up the parts of main façades; at Versailles the scale became so massive that a new, simple treatment had to be employed.

The effect of the influence of this great Baroque palace cannot be restricted simply to other palaces; its impact was felt in many spheres, in the layout of towns, in the detail designs of parks and gardens for rulers and merchants and in the decoration of public buildings. Karlsruhe in Germany, L'Enfant's plan for Washington, St Petersburg, Potsdam, Copenhagen and, quite possibly, Blenheim in England, are within its sphere.

Versailles had expressed the common unity of the arts but soon after the middle of the eighteenth century a reaction had set in against the Baroque. By this time, too, the flag of absolutism was flying low and a new liberal consciousness was emerging in a world of individualism and

The Hall of Mirrors by Mansart is the most sumptuous part of the Palace of Versailles.

In India, with its own traditions in architecture, we find on the soil of New Delhi a monumental palace based on the Classical style which was built for the viceroy by Sir Edgar Lutyens.

confused ideals. Scientific archaeology was growing and with it the definitions of classicism based on the first-hand research of the connoisseurs and scholars. Architectural copy-books were produced in abundance and quickly transmitted ideas from country to country. The Classical Revival held sway in Europe until the end of the century, when an equally scholarly interest in medievalism grew up.

A choice of styles

With the new liberalism, a desire had arisen for national identity. Nationalism was to find its expression in architectural terms through great public buildings. The social purpose of architecture was given a new twist and buildings were to become the new symbols of democratic government.

In the nineteenth century classicism was soon to crumble under the pressure of the new Romanticism that gripped Europe after 1830. The architectural situation was fluid and designers worked within the confines of known past styles including the classical, the medieval, the Romanesque and so on, as mood and conviction dictated. There seems to have been little logic behind Charles Barry's choice of the Gothic style for the principal palace of British government, the Houses of Parliament. It could equally well have been classical. However, because it was Gothic inspiration, it spawned similar government buildings throughout the British Empire. Similarly the United States Capitol in Washington proved proto-typical for many later public buildings in that country and abroad; as America found its ideals tied to those of Greece and Rome, its new democratic buildings reflected this attitude.

It was in the countries where the 'new architecture' mainly came to birth that, paradoxically, restrictions were introduced to stunt its growth. The freedom of the post-revolutionary Constructivists, architects and designers, in Russia was curtailed in the early 1930s; German experimentalism ended in 1933 and was replaced by Nazi classicism; Italian rationalism was cut short by Mussolini's concept of a New Rome. Neo-classicism reappeared at this time under the guise of political acceptability.

Adolf Hitler, who included among his maniacal tendencies a desire to become a great architect, imposed dictates for a thoroughly Teutonic architecture. The Führer demanded a rational architecture. 'To be German', he said, 'is to be logical.' His two main architects were Paul Troost (who died in 1934) and Albert Speer, who was responsible for the development of greater Berlin and for the building of the Reichskanzlei (Chancellery), the new centre of political power. This building,

The art gallery in Munich was built in the severe neo-classical style of National Socialism.

Punjab. His advice was sought, and ostensibly rejected, although his sketches were used, for the design of the United Nations tower building in New York, and he was the inspiration behind the new civic and parliamentary buildings at Brazilia. Le Corbusier was, in a very real sense, an architect of Caesar, an authoritarian designer with great humanitarian ideals, yet a modern technological man as well. His palaces (for even his private houses possess a palatial quality) have a timeless symbolism that is characteristic of all great building.

with its long, rambling plan, was like the early Greek 'Citadel Palaces'. Its chief rooms led off internal courtyards and the whole was secure against intruders.

However, it was not simply Hitler who curtailed the development of a new public architecture. In 1927 Le Corbusier was awarded a prize in the Palace of the League of Nations Competition (Geneva) and four years later in the competition for its Communist counterpart, the Palace of the Soviets. Both of these designs were promptly rejected. Although these buildings were never built, their designs were clearly based on the economy of means expressed in early Greek palaces and on the proportional arrangement of the Renaissance Palazzi. Also, they were functionally modern and distinguished in their spatial arrangements and utilitarian aim.

Little that follows Le Corbusier's work in the latter years of this century offers anything new. He seems to have expressed for most younger architects the ideals of twentieth-century humanism. His own designs were used for the legislative building of Chandigahr, the new capital of the

The United Nations headquarters in New York was designed by an international committee. The towering block of the Secretariat Building has been a powerful influence on the style of subsequent high buildings.

Keeping the enemy out

The great civilizations of the world have developed through cross-fertilization with others, often through war and conquest. In this context, fortifications have exerted a decisive influence.

THE TOWER, or keep, is the main expression of military architecture. It served as a look-out and also gave the defenders a decided advantage over those attacking at ground level. Before artillery and firearms were perfected, weapons were restricted to the bow and arrow (and cross-bow), lance, battering ram and giant catapults. The tower, wall and moat were the principal means of defence. Until the Turks developed efficient cannon in the fifteenth century, the enemy approaching by land or water could be kept at bay by relatively simple systems using these three elements.

Herod's refuge

The Romans established a large empire and built very extensively. There are remains of their military works throughout Europe, the Levant and North Africa. Roman camps built for the sieges of cities became so perfectly planned that they were used as models for new cities. They were rectangular enclosures, usually with four gates: the main gate, the *Porta Praetoria,* led to the commanding officer's tent or *praetorium.* Walls were strengthened by towers, alternating with machines for throwing stones and other missiles. One of the earliest permanent fortifications is the Italian city of Aosta, built by Augustus in 23 A D.

Some of the finest military works of the early Christian era were built under the Herods by the Jews. Herod the Great took Jerusalem in 37 B C and raised and strengthened the walls. In 30 B C he built a fortress at Masada as a personal refuge against the Roman occupation of Jerusalem. This fortress stands on a plateau, capping a high hill close to the west shore of the Dead Sea. It has steep approaches all around and is inaccessible except by a narrow, winding path from the west. Like many castles of the Middle Ages, it was built entirely as an isolated fortress for the defence of one leader and his followers, at a time when other strongholds were intended for the protection of large communities.

The Romans first invaded Britain in 55 B C, but it was not until 43 A D that the conquest was consolidated by the construction of a system of military roads and forts. This system centred on the legionary British forts at York, Chester and Caerleon, and the towns founded at Colchester, Leicester and elsewhere. Almost 40 years later, Agricola established a northern boundary, with a chain of forts across the isthmus between the Forth and the Clyde in Scotland.

Between 122 and 125 a continuous wall, known as Hadrian's Wall, was built on the north side of these camps. This wall was 73 miles long and for most of its length

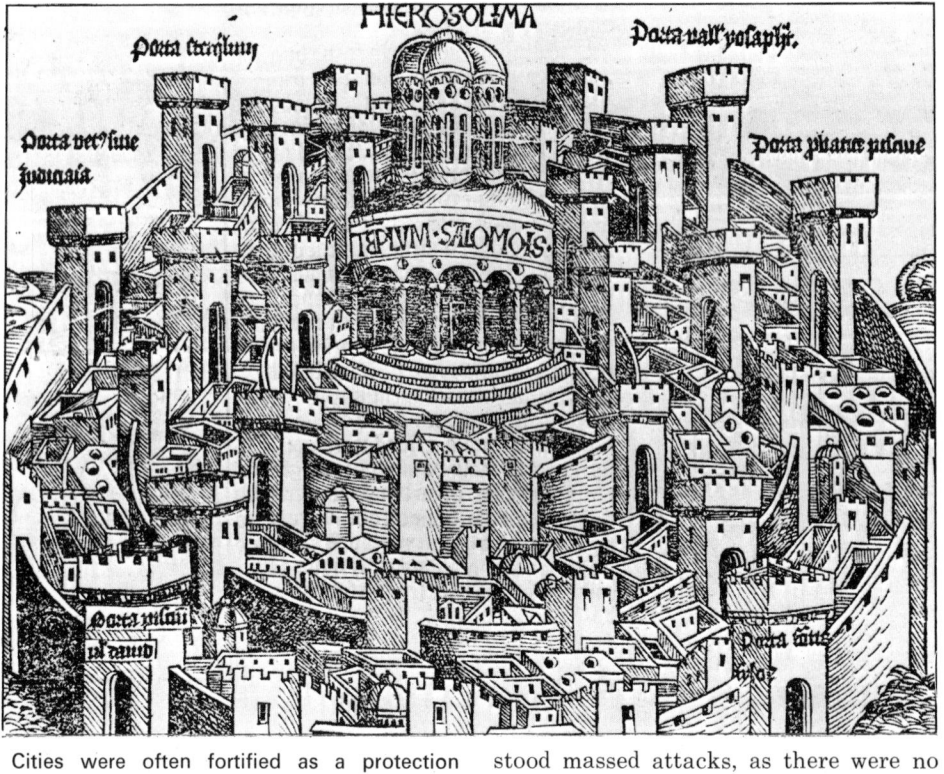

Cities were often fortified as a protection against enemies. Herod the Great took Jerusalem in 37 BC and strengthened the walls. The Crusaders conquered it in 1099. This woodcut is from the *Nuremburg Chronicles* of 1493.

7 ft 6 in. thick. Originally 20 ft high, it was built mainly along the tops of high ridges, providing a sharp fall on the north side. Where the wall straddles lower ground it is defended by a deep ditch, with a flat terrace or berm between ditch and wall.

There were 17 camps at about 4-mile intervals. At every Roman mile along the Wall there is a mile-castle, a rectangular building projecting south of the wall; signal turrets form subdivisions between the mile-castles. A 20-ft-wide road to the south of the Wall connected all the stations. The Wall could not have with-

stood massed attacks, as there were no access stairways between the stations, mile-castles and signal turrets, but it was a deterrent and provided a continuous sentry-walk along the border.

After the Gallic wars of 58–49 BC, the Romans built their own system of military headquarters throughout Gaul, and extensive remains can still be seen at Fréjus, Nîmes, Autun, Le Mans and Senlis. Fréjus was founded in 31 BC and was an important naval station and harbour. Among the interesting remains is the *Porte des Gaulles,* set in a large, semi-circular forecourt, the entrance guarded on either side by powerful round towers. The gate itself is flanked by towers, and there are three entrances, the central one for carriages and the others for pedestrians.

Perhaps the finest fortifications of the

left to defend themselves against invaders. The struggles that followed allowed no time for the development of scientific fortifications in the West, but there were developments in the Eastern, or Byzantine Empire. In 413, to protect Constantinople against the Huns, a wall was built across the land side of the promontory on which the city stands. It was strengthened every 60 yards by large towers. A moat and an outer wall enclosing it were added in 477. The fortifications of Nicaea in Asia Minor follow the design of the Constantinople land walls in enclosing the city.

After the Vandals had been defeated by the East-Roman general Belisarius (533–534 A D), fortifications were built throughout the newly acquired territories of North Africa. They included fortified towns like Guelma, Thelepte and Bagai; open towns with fortified citadels – Haidra, Mdauroch and Timgad; and isolated fortresses such as Lemsa and Ain Tounga. The first two categories served as military stations and refuges for the civilian popu-

Masada, the refuge of a jewish sect when the Romans occupied Jerusalem in 70 A D, was built on a high plateau above the Dead Sea The design resembles plans of medieval castles

latter days of the Roman Empire are the walls of Rome. Aurelian (270–275 A D) defeated the Goths, overthrew Tetricus, the pretender to the throne, in Gaul and restored the empire to its former limits. He also improved military discipline and extended the confines of Rome, surrounding it with a 12-ft-thick wall, and enclosing the *Castra Praetoria* within the city.

The Roman Empire in the West was at an end by 476. Roman legions were withdrawn from the outposts of the Western Empire and formerly captive nations were

Aurelian, Roman emperor from 270 to 275, strengthened Rome by building a wall 12 miles long and 12 ft thick. It is depicted here in the *Très Riches Heures du Duc de Berry*.

lation; the last were placed in strategic defensive positions.

The Normans introduced their own system of fortifications into England following the Conquest of 1066. Known as the motte and bailey it consisted of a mound (motte) 10–100 ft high and 100–300 ft in diameter, and areas surrounding the motte (baileys or wards). Both the motte and baileys were circled by ditches. This system is found in Germany, Italy and Denmark, but is most prevalent in Normandy and England. The mounds were of three types: natural hillocks; part natural and part artificial; completely artificial. If the mound were completely artificial, it

Rectangular donjons, or keeps, based on Roman and Byzantine examples, were introduced into Europe around 1070. The White Tower, part of the Tower of London, was the first.

could support only timber defences on its summit. An example was discovered at Abinger in Surrey. Prior Laurence, writing of Durham about 1150, describes the typical stone keep with timber internal partitions. There are many of these 'shell-keeps' in England, dating from the eleventh and twelfth centuries. Tamworth (with a polygonal plan) and Launceston (with an oval plan) are good examples.

The shell-keep was gradually supplanted by the rectangular keep or donjon. These followed Roman and Byzantine examples and were strong and convenient. They were introduced into England around 1070, the White Tower of the Tower of London being the first, followed by Canterbury and Colchester. They were generally built on the firm ground of the bailey. They had two to four storeys, thick walls (usually buttressed) and the entrance, at the second storey, was reached by a stairway. The principal or 'great' hall was on the entrance floor and often had a gallery above, with chambers and latrines opening off. There was usually a chapel and a well. Roofs were often of timber and vulnerable to enemy missiles so the keep walls were carried up high above the gutters for protection. There was a postern for escape in case the enemy took the main entrance.

At the Council of Clermont in 1095, Pope Urban II summoned Western Christendom to liberate Eastern Christians, and the first crusader army assembled beneath the walls of Constantinople in the winter of 1096–7. In the spring they crossed the Hellespont (now the Bosphorus) and marched on Nicaea. In their eastward progress the Frankish forces encountered many massive Byzantine fortifications which were without equal in Europe at that time. Jerusalem was taken in July 1099 and the Frankish knights then set out from the Holy City to enlarge their domain in Palestine. In contrast to the older fortifications which the Franks had taken over, their new castles were essentially offensive

Krak des Chevaliers in Syria was built on a hilltop 100 ft high with steep gradients on all sides. It has two concentric rings of fortifications linked by a long ramp for horsemen.

bases. Most of them were placed in strategic and well-protected positions, near major caravan routes or beside large towns. They followed the Byzantine and Arab castles in conforming to local topography and exploiting the terrain. They normally consisted of a donjon surrounded by a system of walls and towers. Krak des Chevaliers, a castle and village in southern Syria, is of particular interest.

Experience in the Levant had shown that hilltops were the best sites for forts, if they could be protected by several lines of walls. Back in Europe such developments from 1190 to 1280 were dominated by the round donjon. Among the first was Château Gaillard in France. It was built by Richard I of England on a 300-ft cliff above the Seine. It had three baileys, the inner one on the edge of the cliff, with a moat between the middle and inner baileys. The two outer walls had circular wall-towers and the circular donjon had a thicker wall on the courtyard side, shaped like the prow of a ship, facing the direction most vulnerable to the battering ram and missiles. Entrance was effected by a flight of steps from the courtyard to the upper storey. The donjon at Coucy in France is the largest and strongest and most magnificent of all the medieval round towers. It was built between 1230 and 1250 and was 160 ft high. Pembroke, although only a third of the size of Coucy, is probably the best example in Britain.

The reign of Edward I (1272–1307) saw the development of a typical English fortress. Edward, a soldier king who had experience of the Crusades in Syria (1271–2) and had fought the Welsh and the Scots, favoured a concentric fortress with several

The thirteenth-century fortifications of Carcassonne in France, perched high on a hill, consist of a double line of ramparts protected at frequent intervals by towers.

terrain. The Rhine Valley has many powerful fortresses. A classic example is Marksburg near Braubach, with a central tower developed from a Romanesque original. It has small, homely rooms with grand titles like the Hall of the Knights, and the hanging turrets are of French style. The fortresses of the Upper Palatinate were less picturesque because they were more exposed to heavy battles.

The utilization of natural terrain is not as apparent in Italy as it is in Germany. A standard type of fortress is to be found on mountain tops, but picturesque groupings such as prevail in Germany are rare. German work influenced the fortress at Caminate, with its turret and comfortable quarters, and Soave in the province of Verona is German in its basic design. The towered fortress, although not perfected as in Normandy, is a significant part of Italian military work up to the end of the Middle Ages. Until that time there were turret fortresses on all the Italian coasts. and the tower retained its hold on provincial forts. Frederick II retained the tower tradition; his most personal fortress was the Castel del Monte in Apulia.

The fortress at Pembroke in Wales was constructed by the Normans, about 1090. The circular, 75-ft-high donjon was added in 1200.

defence lines and single turrets. These forts could be captured step by step, since each turret could hold out individually. Edward I began a series of large constructions that were continued by his son Edward II (1307–27) and his grandson Edward III (1327-77). Caerphilly, begun in 1267 and completed by Edward I, was Britain's largest fortress. The design was typically concentric, with double wall belts, massive corner towers, and gates with towers that are fortresses in themselves. They were built primarily as military strongholds, with only one hall and some dwellings on the south side. In the 1280s this style reached its peak at Conway, Caernarvon and Harlech.

The fortresses of Germany and her border regions present the most varied collection of military architecture in Europe, resulting mainly from the individual character of the small states. But their variety of form is based on clearly defined principal types. The first and most important of these is the wall system adapted to the

28

The development of artillery after the Turks took Constantinople in 1453 demanded a different approach to fortifications. In 1494, when Charles VIII of France marched through Italy, his cannon reduced Italian forts with astounding rapidity. But early cannon were fixed in their cradles and could not be wall-mounted in order to dip and fire on those below. It was not until the end of the fifteenth century

In 1521 Suleyman the Magnificent captured Belgrade in Hungary for the Turks, who made it the chief fortress in Europe. The town is depicted in a sixteenth-century Turkish miniature.

Fortified castles like Burg Eltz were perched on crags high above the Rhine. Ideally situated for look-out posts, their architecture was particularly well suited to the terrain.

Perpetual strife between the Guelph and the Ghibelline factions produced not only communal fortifications but private towers within towns. San Germignano is an outstanding example, with 20 such towers in this relatively small town 20 miles northwest of Siena. Thirteen remain today, seven of them grouped around the main piazza. Individual palaces were also fortified and had bold towers, like the Palazzo Vecchio in Florence, begun in 1298. In the fifteenth and sixteenth centuries palaces became less fortified and more decorative. Perhaps the most picturesque of Italian sixteenth-century castles is that by Baldassare Peruzzi at Roccasinibalda. The castle rises sheer from the floor of the valley, and its plan is in the form of an eagle.

Walmer Castle, one of a line of forts built by Henry VIII, has a quatrefoil base of one storey and a central circular tower rising two further storeys.

that gunloops began to appear in fortifications. From about 1540, residential quarters were separated from military structures in Britain, with the almost undefended manor house on the one hand and the king's fort on the other.

Henry's forts

During the reign of Henry VIII there was great progress in military works and many old castles were reconditioned and strengthened. As Henry had broken with the pope and was at variance with the emperor, he might expect an invasion at any moment. He therefore built a line of artillery forts along the south coast of England. The main design principle was that the whole building should be concentrated into a compact block which could be defended all round by artillery, the gun emplacements rising in tiers one

behind the other. Deal is one of the largest of these forts, and has a sexfoil plan. Walmer is similar but simpler, with a quatrefoil base. In these forts of Henry VIII the perfect symmetry of Edward I's forts is echoed, with even stronger utilitarian purpose.

The rapid improvements of firearms in the sixteenth century meant that fortifications had to be kept lower. In most cases towns were the initiators of the defence systems and responsible for modernizations. Methods of defence became more international. Defence systems were moved as far as possible forward from the castle itself, and the keep lost its original function. The striving for innovation was expressed in elaborate ramparts and bastions: an independent 'line' in front of the main fortifications, and defences became more ornamental than functional. Fortresses became redundant and fell into disrepair. With the coming of railways, aircraft and tanks, war was no longer concerned with fixed installations.

Architecture's basic bones

Stonehenge stands as a monument to the durability of post and beam construction. The oldest device known to architecture, it still plays an essential part in buildings of today.

ANCIENT LEGEND has it that the imposing monoliths at Stonehenge were transported from Ireland by the wizard Merlin. Modern theories state otherwise, for it is thought that the upright structures, brought from as far as 150 miles away were manoeuvred into place by toppling them into holes, while great mounds of earth were built to drag horizontal slabs up on top of them.

Apollo of the Hyperboreans

Whatever you choose to believe, it is certain that these monuments are a striking early example of a type of construction that is called post and lintel construction, where independent horizontal members span vertical supports. This is one of the most basic forms of building known to Man, and it has persisted in one form or another over thousands of years down to the present day. Structures derived from this basic one have continuous horizontal members spanning their supports and are known as post and beam constructions, while those whose supports are continuous through several storeys are called frame constructions. They are all jointly termed trabeated constructions.

Stonehenge dates back as far as 2000 BC

and was preceded, archaeologists believe, by the Woodhenges, wooden structures which perished long ago. The existence of Stonehenge was known to the Greek historian Hecateus in the sixth century BC, who refers to it as the great circular temple of Apollo of the Hyperboreans, a

Stonehenge, earliest extant example in Britain of the most elementary form of building, known as post and lintel construction, where two upright structures support a horizontal.

legendary people whose name the Greeks interpreted as meaning 'Beyond the North Wind'. Apollo, amongst his many functions, was the sun god, and from Hecateus's statement it seems that Stonehenge was the centre of a sun cult. Communications between Great Britain and the Mediterranean were sufficiently good for him to have a fairly accurate idea of the building and its purpose. This is corroborated by the discovery in Salisbury Plain of ancient Egyptian beads, perhaps used as barter, dating from about 1300 B C. Archaeologists conjecture from this evidence that as far back as 4,000 years ago, Britain supported a society sufficiently developed to commission, conceive and execute a building like this.

The technique of handling and raising the large blocks of stone that were used at Stonehenge was probably learnt from Crete. Britain was in fact a principal supplier of tin to the Mediterranean and therefore an important trading post in Bronze Age Europe. She had already

The ancient Egyptian temple of King Zoser is a stone copy of an even earlier timber frame building with mud-brick infill.

acquired from the Mediterranean during the Old Stone Age the techniques of agriculture. Without agriculture there could be no settled communities and therefore no society which was elaborately differentiated into professions, and thus no architects or builders.

It is likely that most early trabeated architectures such as those of ancient Egypt, ancient Greece and central America duplicated in stone forms which were originally developed for construction in wood. Timber is quite strong in tension, which means that a timber beam can withstand a considerable vertical load without fracture; this is why our floors are still usually made of timber. But it is an organic material liable to destruction by fire, fungus and vermin. In addition it is not very dimensionally stable, since it swells and warps with variations in atmospheric humidity.

Stone is brittle

As timber grew scarcer, a new material had to take its place. Stone also lasts longer and is more dimensionally stable, features especially important for a building like Stonehenge, which seems to have been used for making astronomical observations for calendars.

Unlike timber, stone is rather brittle, and instead of bending under a vertical load it suddenly yields by fracturing. (This process going on below the Earth's crust is probably responsible for earthquakes.) In addition, the weight required for a given strength must be much higher than in the case with wood. On the other hand, it can be obtained in far larger sizes. During the annual Nile flood, the agricultural ancient Egyptians had an enormous surplus labour force. They were able to put several hundred thousand men to work on the building of the Great Pyramid for several decades as a sort of compulsory unemployment relief, and rapidly evolved constructions of over-

The Palace of Minos in Knossos on Crete was built long ago in prehistoric times. It was re-constructed at the beginning of this century in plaster and concrete. The columns formed like upturned tree-trunks.

powering grandeur. The gigantic columns in some Egyptian temples are monoliths weighing several hundred tons.

The Greeks of the classical period were organized as a series of autonomous city-states living by sea trade. The greater refinement and slighter scale of their buildings are partly due to their restricted labour force and partly to their interest in perspective drawing systems which they were developing at the time in connection with mural and theatrical scene painting.

Theorists in the eighteenth century supposed that the Greek schemes of con-struction derived from timber prototypes like those of the Egyptians. Subsequent archaeological research in Crete and at Mycenae and Tiryns in the Peloponnese seems to corroborate this theory; and it was discovered that a very ancient and revered temple at Olympia had its wooden columns gradually replaced by stone ones in late classical times.

Timber perishes relatively quickly, and few buildings in this material last much more than 500 years, so most of the existing timber-framed buildings are no older than that. Timber and masonry constructions of these periods are quite distinct from one another. The Romans perfected a masonry technique based on a form of concrete and builders in the Romanesque and Gothic periods worked with small stones.

In the timber houses of the Middle Ages, as in all trabeated construction except where they are reproduced in stone, the supports and the infill are separate, since the infill exists chiefly to keep the weather out or, in our own day, to let the daylight

The floating *torii* of the island shrine of Miya-jima near Hiroshima, Japan, is a post and lintel construction founded in ancient times, which has to be rebuilt when the timber perishes.

in. The materials used for infilling in the Middle Ages included wattle and daub, which was probably one of the earliest infilling materials, lath and plaster, tiling on battens, and bricks, in addition to lapped boards which are still common in the United States and occasionally occur in England.

The advent of machine saws and planes in about 1800 made timber working much simpler. Whereas the older timber frames required skilled joinery and relied on carefully made joints, the modern balloon frame can be put together floor by floor by nailing the horizontal members to the uprights. It uses essentially standardized wood members straight from the sawmill.

In the eighteenth century, there was an important break-through: means were developed for the large-scale production of cast iron. This began to be used in place of timber, especially in mills, first for the vertical and later for the horizontal members. Cast iron is strong in compression, that is, when it is pushed, but rather brittle, and so a good deal less strong in tension, that is, when pulled.

The medieval tithe barn at Great Coxwell in Berkshire, England. Basically a timber frame building, its supports are, however, provided with brackets which make them into semi-trusses.

Staple Inn in Holborn, London, is a splendid example of a late medieval timber frame building. The infill between the beams is made of lath and plaster.

Hammerbeam roof, Wymondham Abbey in Norfolk, England. Short beams project at right angles from the top of the wall in order to support arched braces.

Unlike wood, however, it is non-inflammable, it is rot and vermin proof, and it is not sensitive to humidity. All these things, together with its vastly superior strength, commended it for constructional work. Shortly after the introduction of cast-iron framing for multi-storey industrial buildings, timber in the floors was replaced by masonry in the form of shallow brick and tile arches spanning between the bottom flanges of parallel iron beams.

Rolled into shape

The production of both iron and steel had gone on since the early Iron Age, but it was an expensive and time-consuming process, and the quality of the product was very variable. The production of steel in quantity began about a hundred years after that of cast iron, with the invention of the Bessemer converter for burning the impurities out of the molten iron. The boat store at Sheerness in Kent, England, was built in 1858–60; a remarkably early example of a cast-iron frame construction.

Unlike cast iron, which is essentially a crystalline, rather brittle material, steel is a malleable material, actually an alloy of iron with small amounts of carbon or other materials, which has to be rolled into the required shape while still red-hot. The resulting members, whatever their shape, can be joined together with bolts and rivets or welded into compound shapes of varying complexity. The production technique is therefore essentially a mechanized extension of the village forge.

As a building material, especially for use in framed constructions, steel came into its own with the reconstruction of Chicago in the 1880s after the great fire. Without it, and the concurrent development of the high-speed elevator and electric lighting, the development of the skyscraper might never have taken place. The last of the tall brick buildings in Chicago, the Monadnock block, is only 16 storeys high, but its walls are nearly six feet thick at the base, totalling hun-

Essentially a plastic material, steel can be moulded into any shape while red-hot. The steel frame members of Crown Hall, Ilinois Institute of Technology, Chicago were welded together. The infill is made of glass.

dreds of square feet in cross-section. A building like the Empire State, 103 storeys and over 1,000 feet high, is carried to its foundations on a total cross-section of a few square feet of steel, arranged in the form of isolated columns, probably of compound 'H' section.

Immensely strong as steel is in both tension and compression, there is an ultimate upper limit, convenience and expense apart, to the height of a building. The major load which all buildings of any size have to carry to ground is their own dead weight, whether they are Egyptian temples with gratuitously over-scaled parts, spare Gothic cathedrals, or modern skyscrapers. A tall building has also to be braced against deflection in wind. However, beyond a certain size, which can be quite simply calculated, any building will collapse under its own dead weight, although this factor depends both on the geometry of the building and also the material of which it is made. Long before this limit is reached the building becomes uneconomic to construct and use. Most of the steelwork in a tall building exists to support the dead weight of the building, and to prevent it overturning in a gale-force wind.

The strength and above all the con-

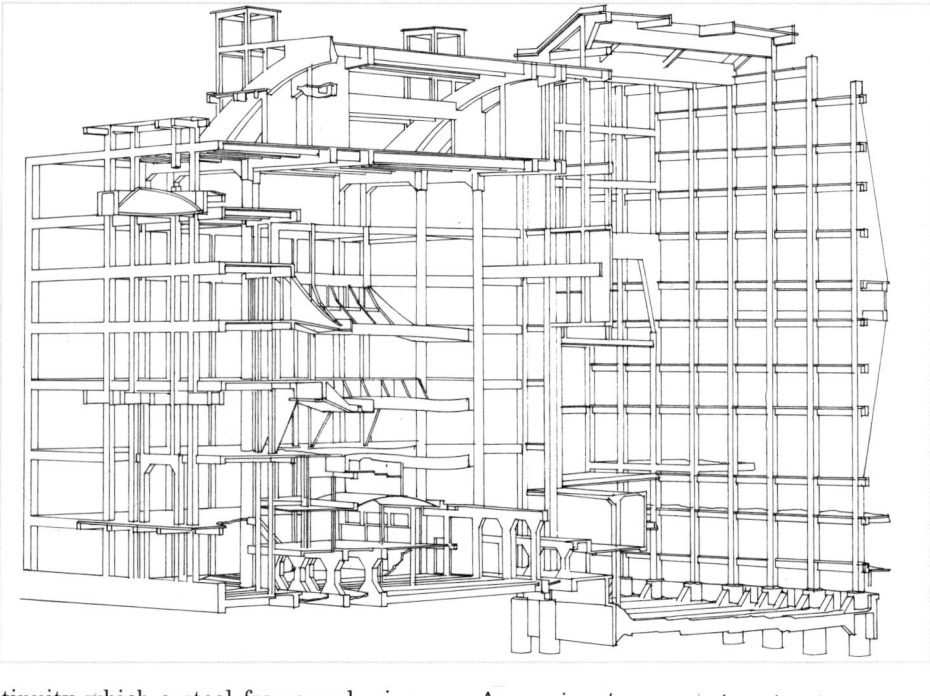

tinuity which a steel framework gives a building is best illustrated by an example: in 1945 a plane crashed into the Empire State Building, leaving a big hole in the wall. The event went almost unnoticed by the occupants, save by a vigilant engineer in the basement who was startled to see that an aero engine had fallen to the bottom of one of the lift shafts, and gave the alarm. In comparable circumstances a light Gothic building like the Cathedral at Beauvais in France would have been extensively shattered, and an Egyptian temple badly dented. A timber-framed building would probably have been badly damaged by fire as well as by the impact.

Steel and concrete

Reinforced-concrete frame construction was developed in Europe, principally in France, shortly after steel-frame construc-

An engineer's perspective drawing of the Théâtre des Champs Elysées, Paris, by Auguste Perret, a reinforced-concrete frame construction.

tion began to be used in the United States. In a loaded beam, which deflects slightly under load, the top of the beam is in compression and the bottom in tension. Stone is too brittle to support much load in tension, but if we incorporate steel bars in concrete, which is a kind of cast stone, and distribute them always where tension will occur, we can rely partly or wholly on the concrete to look after the compression. This is the basic theory underlying reinforced-concrete slabs and beams, and it is possible to maintain the necessary adhesion between the two, because steel and concrete expand by approximately the same amount with rising temperature.

Steelwork arrives in sections of standardized dimension on the building site,

37

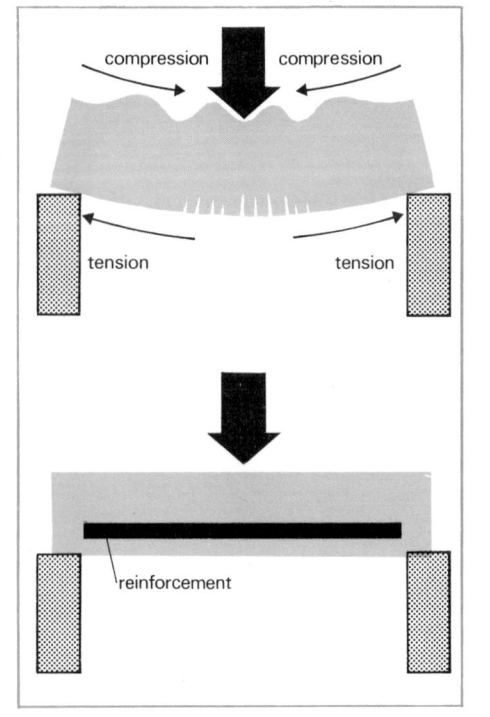

A load pressing down on a beam causes it to be *in compression* (on the top) and *in tension* as it is pulled apart at the bottom. Certain materials are damaged under strain; reinforced concrete is one of the strongest.

and must be joined together to make a framework by bolting, riveting or welding. Concrete, however, is poured between temporary surfaces of wood or other material and left to set, after which the temporary surfaces, known as framework or shuttering, are removed. The fabrication and erection of these temporary casting surfaces can account for as much as 40 per cent of the constructional costs. For this reason, steelwork is more frequently used in large building construction in countries like the United States where labour costs are comparatively more expensive than material costs, and conversely in South America, where steel imported from the United States is expensive owing to freight charges, but labour is cheap. Concrete, however, can be built to a far greater variety of shapes than steel, and for certain classes of construction the drawbacks of the initial construction costs are outweighed by the advantages.

In both steel and reinforced-concrete frames a factor is present which is absent from all other forms of trabeated construction except certain kinds of timber frame, and this is stiffness. Continuity is given to a steel frame by rigid connections between beam and column, especially by means of welding, and to reinforced-concrete frames by the inherent continuity of the reinforcement. This continuity makes the calculation of the sizes more difficult, but brings great economies; for the construction is stiff as a whole and individual parts are not dependent on their own strength alone in resisting deformation under load.

It is characteristic of all forms of frame construction that the function of support and the function of infill are entirely separate and can be solved each in the most convenient and presentable way, whether with ancient mud-brick or modern plate glass.

And so we have seen that timber is likely to have been both the earliest and the prototypical material. It was replaced by the more brittle stone, because until the Industrial Revolution made other more suitable materials available in quantity, it was the only natural material that was much more durable and more dimensionally stable than timber. The ideal materials for trabeated constructions are elastic materials like steel, reinforced concrete and more recently, laminated plastics. These all deflect under load, but when the load is removed, they return to their original shape with their strength unimpaired, like an india-rubber or a car spring.

The vaulting arch

The igloo in the cold far north, the huge dome over St Peter's – both are examples of a kind of building whose development is an exciting testimony to the skill of designers and engineers.

BUILDING WITH THE ARCH AND DOME began long ago in the distant past, nobody is quite sure when. But we do know that the forms are related to primitive huts made out of bent boughs and thatch, to tents, and to huts of mud or ice, forms which survive to the present day. The nomads of central Asia still use domed tents of a hide covering stretched on to a frame of sticks. In the marshes of Iraq, the Arabs build halls of pointed arch construction, made from bundles of tall reeds. In Africa people build very sophisticated domed thatched huts, and in the far north, in the ice deserts where there is no other building material, the Eskimo constructs for his winter quarters a domed hut of ice blocks, carefully cut to fit exactly to each other over a curved surface.

Pushing, not pulling

As a natural material, timber seems to be just right in a strength-to-weight ratio for bridging a wide gap without breaking under its own weight. The breaking force in the middle of a beam is mainly one of tension, of pulling apart. Woods and metals are strong in tension but stone and brick are very weak. The main strength of the latter lies in compression, in their resistance to crushing, and stones and bricks can be built into very large piles before they are crushed by their own weight.

Stones and bricks built into arches are really being piled and balanced one on another, so the force is entirely one of compression. There is no tension in an arch, dome or vault (arched ceiling). All the stones push against one another until

Masjid-i-Shah, the royal mosque, in Isfahan, Persia, has a magnificent corbelled dome, built in rings of diminishing size. The surface is covered in brilliant enamelled tiles.

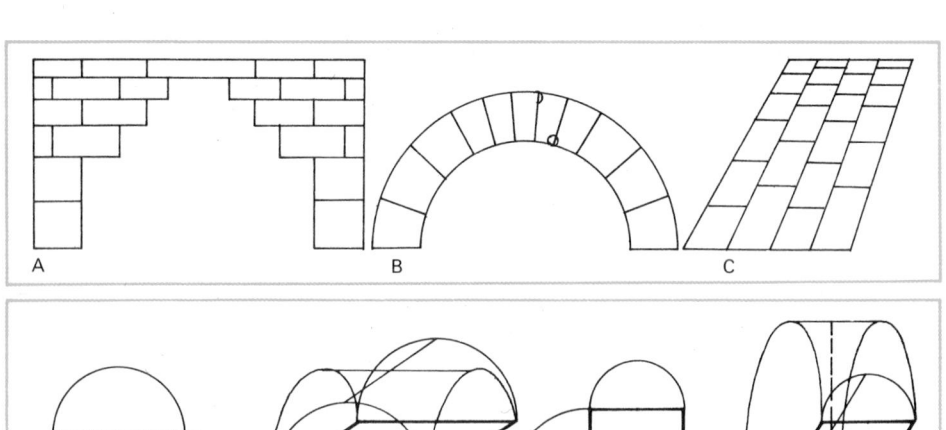

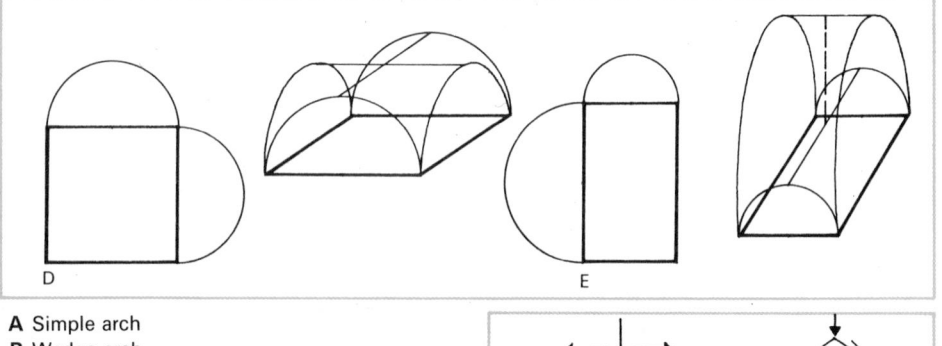

A Simple arch
B Wedge arch
C Earliest wedge arch (side view)
D Cross vaulting on a square
E Attempted cross vaulting on a rectangle
F Semi-circular arch
G Pointed arch

the forces reach the ground. Whatever its natural origins, the arch was developed as a sophisticated building form in those parts of the world where timber for beams and lintels was scarce, that is to say, in the hot, dry countries of the Middle East. Here arches were built of small stones, or mud bricks, at the same time as people were building with the column and beam in ancient Greece.

The first and simplest arches were made by balancing small flat stones one on another, gradually increasing their inward overlapping in small, safe steps (see diagram A). Such a structure is easy and safe to build, and quite stable when finished. It can also be made quite large. In ancient Greece, at a time when temple architecture had reached its familiar form of column and beam, most small houses were still being built in this way, out of small stones or mud bricks.

A more sophisticated form of simple arch is made of specially shaped bricks or stones, cut into wedges (see diagram B). As the tapered stones are forced into the ring by a load exerted upon them, the tighter they are wedged together and the stronger the arch becomes, with one important factor to be considered. As the forces increase downward through the arch, so the forces become bigger and reach their maximum at the bottom where the arch touches the ground. Here the wedging is least, and the forces greatest, and if the load became too great, the stones would fly apart. So a certain mass must be applied on the sides of the arch or dome to hold it together. The earliest wedge arches were made by leaning the brick courses one on another as well as wedging them (see diagram C).

If we rotate an arch through 180 degrees, we have a dome. It is a very useful concept to think of all domes as being arches rotated in this way to form a complete spatial enclosure of their own.

Both the Egyptians and the Greeks knew about the arch and dome, and used them for drains, sewers, small houses, granaries, stores and so on. They preferred the column and lintel for official architecture like palaces and temples, for social and religious rather than technological reasons.

It was the Romans who really developed the arch and dome into sound engineering forms on a large scale. They used timber scaffolding, known as centering, to support enormous arches and domes under construction. Their building material was a kind of light, strong concrete known as *puozzolana*. This was a mixture of lime and prepared volcanic *tufa,* or pumice. Chemists have analysed this material, but the method of preparation is not known with certainty today.

Into this mass of cement, builders inserted layers of flat, tile-like bricks. Arches of interlocking clay pots and pipes combining lightness with strength were also set into the concrete. The shuttering or formwork, the temporary frame into which the wet concrete was poured, was lined with brick, which became a permanent skin on the building, and this in turn was covered with a decorative architectural layer of stone. The Romans fully exploited the advantage that arches have over beams, namely that they are able to bridge vastly greater gaps. The Roman building known as the Pantheon remained the largest single enclosed space in the world for 19 centuries.

The Pantheon at Rome is made of a mass of rammed earth, brick and concrete, with a huge hole over 30 feet across in the middle of the roof – a giant hut in conception.

The Pantheon, the giant bath halls and basilicas of the late Roman Empire were held together by sheer mass, the thickness of the walls resisting the outward pressure at the base of the arches. In Byzantium, where Roman technology was married to Greek thought and ingenuity, the dome of the great church of Sta Sophia was supported by transferring the thrust to half domes built round the main dome. These formed separate arched buttresses which carried out the same function as a solid mass, but economized in materials and added useful space inside.

The various invading tribes of Celts, German and Huns, who together with rebellious slaves took over the ruins of the Roman Empire, were so much struck with the size and splendour of the buildings that in Britain the Anglo-Saxon invaders thought that Roman York must have been the work of giants.

As Europe gradually recovered, an attempt was made to continue the Roman

The Romans invented the aqueduct, a channel for carrying water. The Segovia Aqueduct in Spain is built of semi-circular wedged arches on solid masonry supports.

Looking down the nave of Ely Cathedral in Cambridgeshire, England, one can see two types of arch. Along the sides are semi-circular Romanesque arches based on Roman models, while bridging the nave are pointed broken arches.

tradition in building. But without Roman organization, without concrete, and without the vast reserves of slave labour, the scale and concept of building was forced to change. A different type of architecture developed, a style which is known as Romanesque (called Norman in England).

This is based on the Roman semi-circular arch extended into a long tunnel. These barrel vaults, as the tunnels are known, were built of cut and wedged stones, carried on walls built of a thick skin of dressed stones filled in with smaller stones and rubble. The buildings were long and tall, but the spans of the vaults were far more limited than the spans of those made of Roman concrete. The thrust of the centre, main vault was supported by smaller, lower vaults on either side. This type of construction gives us a triple-aisled hall with the centre supported on columns, the outer walls being of massive stone with small windows set into them.

High arches or low

The use of semi-circular arches has its own peculiar problems in vaulting and cross-vaulting. If we build such an arch on each wall of a compartment, that compartment must have walls of equal length in order to have all the arches the same height. If one wall is longer than the other, that arch will be correspondingly higher, and it will be extremely difficult to roof the vault in (see diagram D).

Building entirely in multiples of squares is limiting, and a building conference in Durham, England, in the twelfth century seems to have offered the solution to the problem of vaulting over rectangular spaces by suggesting the use of pointed, or broken arches instead of semi-circular ones. The designer could make his arches any height he wished, instead of being limited to the fixed ratio of arch to wall.

There is another, equal advantage which might quite as easily have originated the pointed arch. The top of a semi-circular arch is comparatively flat and the load exerts a strong sideways thrust. With a steep, pointed arch, the thrust is transferred down through the stones in their strongest dimension almost immediately (see diagram E). So pointed arches could be wider or higher than the semi-circular arch, and did not need such massive buttressing. Thus at Durham in 1133, diagonal semi-circular ribs across the vaults were combined with pointed arches on the sides of the vaults, all the intersecting at one point.

Later, the diagonal ribs were also made of pointed arches, and the architecture known as Gothic developed. All Gothic arches are made up of broken circular arches. Until the seventeenth century,

architects and builders had only simple compasses for drawing, or the large-scale equivalent: pegs and ropes. But by breaking the arches into two arcs intersecting at a point, the crown, its weakest part, was strengthened, and the pointed vault approximated closely to the curve known as the *catenary*. This is the curve taken by a hanging string or chain, its two ends held fairly close together. Such a curve when turned upside down forms an arch. This arch is stable and has little outward thrust, since the catenary curve is steep with the ends comparatively close together, and not a flat, shallow dish-like curve with the ends pulled apart.

The Gothic structure became a light,

Borromini's Church of S. Ivo della Sapienza in Rome is built on a six-pointed star shape, the geometry of which is carried up into the vault in a spiralling cupola.

ribbed stone frame. Often the skin over the vaults was only a few inches thick. The outer walls themselves were formed of stone columns and piers (solid masonry supports), and the spaces between them were filled in with glass. A good example of the whole system is the choir of Westminster Abbey, London. This type of architecture in its various developments dominated the European scene from the thirteenth to the late fifteenth century.

Meanwhile, in the early fifteenth century in Italy there had been a revival of interest in Roman architecture, of which there was a great deal still about in the form of gigantic ruins. These revealed the

Brunelleschi's Renaissance ribbed dome over the Pazzi Chapel in Florence is basically a ring of pointed stone arches converging at the crown.

cross-section of Roman arches and vaults, but the secret of making concrete had been lost, and the Renaissance imitators of Roman architecture had to develop new engineering and building techniques. They used the Gothic development of ribbing in a new way.

The Renaissance dome originated from a ring of stone arches converging at the crown, just as the lines of longitude on a globe of the northern hemisphere converge at the Pole. The spaces between the ribs radiating out from the crown were filled with stone slabs. This is called a ribbed dome, and was built on an enormous scale on the cathedral in Florence by Brunelleschi. There is a very beautiful smaller example by the same architect on his Pazzi Chapel, also in Florence.

As we have seen, arches and domes under load tend to flatten at the crown and bulge at the sides. The ribs of a ribbed dome would spread and the filling between them would fall away. The Renaissance architects restrained their domes from splitting open by tying them, so to speak, with a belt around their waist. Brunelleschi did this with his octagonal dome on Florence Cathedral, Michelangelo used it on the dome on St Peter's in Rome, and Wren for his dome on St Paul's Cathedral in London.

The belt in each case consists of one or more forged iron chains carried right round the dome just above the springing, which is where the dome begins to curve inwards from the vertical. The iron is strong in tension, the stone filling strong in compression, so material and forces balance each other.

The introduction of cast iron in the middle eighteenth century, pioneered at Coalbrookdale in Shropshire, England, made arch construction in iron possible. The early cast-iron bridges, like the famous one at Coalbrookdale, have a circular arched form and are made of a great many elements put together with iron

An early cast-iron bridge at Coalbrookdale in Shropshire, England is composed of many parts fixed together with iron rods and wedges.

rods and wedges, most of which are being squeezed ('compressed' in engineering parlance), not pulled apart. The introduction of steel 100 years after cast iron, made it possible for designers to work with arches much wider, flatter and slighter than any ever built before.

The wonderful bridges in the Massif Central in France, built by the great engineer Eiffel for the French State Railways, show something of the extraordinary lightness and vast span which can be obtained with steel. At about the

The Palm House at Kew Gardens in London was designed by Decimus Burton and Richard Turner. Essentially a simple tunnel vault, it is made of standardized parts of glass and cast iron.

Richard Buckminster-Fuller's geodesic domes are composed of five-sided or six-sided elements of steel or aluminium. He designed the U.S. pavilion for Expo '67 in Montreal.

same time, that is in 1887, the engineers Contamin and Dutert erected the famous Hall of Machines, destroyed in 1911, at the Paris International Exhibition. This hall was made of wide, rather flat, lattice-work steel arches, 475 feet wide by 150 feet high. Beauvais Cathedral in France, the highest Gothic building ever built, was only 158 feet high, and it partially collapsed twice after being built. It was a very narrow building in comparison with the Hall of Machines.

'Hydraulic cement'

The transition from cast iron to steel was not sudden and in railway stations such as King's Cross in London (designed by Lewis Cubitt, and built in 1851–2) cast iron is used for members near the supports which are subject to pure compression, while riveted wrought iron, which is malleable and has characteristics much more like steel, is used for members which are going to be

pulled as well as pushed.

Concrete was rediscovered in the late eighteenth century by the Englishman William Smeaton. He called it 'hydraulic cement', since it will set hard under water. The crushing strength of stone was combined with the pulling qualities of steel in the invention of reinforced concrete, which began to be used in building about 15 years after steel. The bridges of the Swiss engineer Robert Maillart are often similar in form to those in iron and steel by Eiffel. But where Eiffel had to build up his bridges from a large number of angles and flats riveted together to get the shape he wanted, Maillart could cast his concrete to the exact form he required.

In recent years, the development of vast vaults and domes in very thin shells of reinforced concrete two or three inches thick has been paralleled by the development of comparably thin domes like those of the American designer Buckminster-Fuller, which are hemispherical and entirely made up of hexagonal and pentagonal elements. These use very little material and can cover enormous spans. At present they are always hemispherical.

'... of clay and wattles made'

Every culture has a customary form of architecture uniquely suited to its environment, and today specialists are discovering in full the potential such forms offer in modern design.

EVERY YEAR, many people leave their homes and take a holiday 'to get away from it all'. Some of them find their leisure in hotels and on sandy beaches; others, however, prefer to stay on a farm, rent a cottage in the country, or go camping. And there will be some who will go even further afield. The reasons for their respective choices may be varied but many will be seeking to avoid the urban environment of congested roads, high density housing and office blocks, to enjoy instead the human scale and the pleasure of living in small communities of humble buildings.

Patterns of behaviour

It is easy to romanticize about 'the simple life', and unrealistic perhaps for sophisticated people to wish away the modern environment and exchange it for one of primitive technology and rudimentary sanitation. Yet the 'cottage in the country'; the 'converted farmhouse in the South of France', is the alternative home the city-dweller obtains, if he can afford it. It may well be that in his choice of retreats the urban dweller and the suburban commuter reveals important truths about the kinds of environment most suited to the human condition.

Ours is a period of regional development of city planning and of new towns. It is a period when the total environment is being designed by specialists whose job it is to balance the needs of communities and families with the amenities, the services and the mobility which the modern environment demands. But planners are not infallible and they may overlook those patterns of behaviour which matter to the people for whom they design but which are little known or understood by them. This is evident in the errors that have been made by planners who have designed for communities in countries of which they had no personal knowledge. Although there have been planned societies before, and towns conceived and built by planners in the past, the extent of architecturally designed building and planned communities has never been on the scale it is at present. Nevertheless, only a small percentage of the world's population today lives in houses designed by architects or in towns built to the designs of planners. The history of 'architecture' is, in fact, the history of buildings designed by specialists. It ignores the greater proportion of Man's varied built environments: the houses, dwellings and buildings of millions of people in Africa, Asia, the Americas, even in Europe, which are 'vernacular', that is, indigenous to the localities where they appear.

Kano, the ancient walled city of northern Nigeria, has a unique form of architecture. The walls of the houses, which are solid and cool, are made of balls of mud.

Vernacular architecture is often considered to be 'primitive', and by the standards of modern industrialized techniques it may often be so. It is evident, however, that building with, for example, a steel-frame construction, may be prohibitively expensive if the resources are not available and transport long and difficult. This would be true even today of places in regions as far apart as British Columbia, Sikkim or Upper Volta – expensive and inappropriate. In such countries the natural resources of timber, mud or grass are immediately available and are employed for building in a manner appropriate to the climate and environment.

Unlike formal architecture, vernacular building arises out of the precise needs of a people in terms of what purpose they want their buildings to serve. In some instances, these buildings may have a symbolic value which is more powerful than their utilitarian one, but more often vernacular buildings illustrate the resources of a district and reflect the society and environmental conditions very precisely. We may see how a particular community shapes its buildings to meet the demands of its social structure; we may learn how material resources have been used and made to work for building needs by the development of an appropriate technology; we may see how the conditions of climate and weather have been countered and accommodated; and we may learn how the terrain, the means of obtaining or producing food and other aspects of environment and behaviour, may exercise controls on the building and determine its form. In this way we may also learn much about our own approach to architecture and building.

Many vernacular forms might illustrate these aspects. The igloo, the winter snow house of the Eskimo, is a remarkable example of a highly intelligent use of natural resources in an inhospitable environment. When on a seal hunt, Eskimos of the Arctic have no access to timber, minerals or stone, but they have an inexhaustible supply of one easily mined material, compressed snow. Their tools are small – carved bone or ivory – but with a bone knife the Eskimo nomad can hew out blocks of snow with skill and speed. The blocks from which the igloo is made are approximately two feet long and slightly tapered in a form which long tradition has refined and determined. The sections are laid in a circular plan upon the snow bed in a gentle and inward leaning spiral. The chinks between the blocks are filled with soft snow and the spiral continues until the blocks assume a dome shape. When the Eskimo has almost completed his spiral he cuts a final wedge-

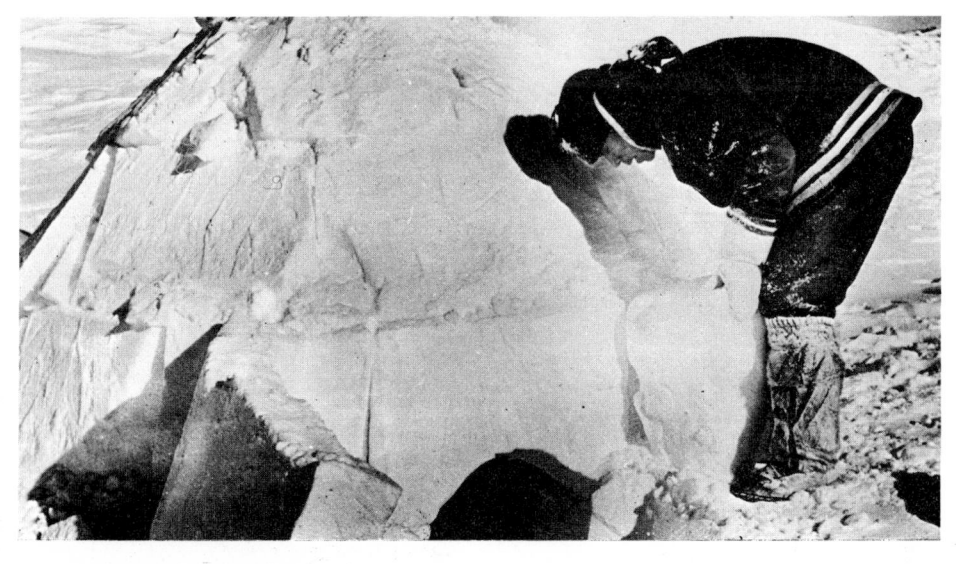

For the Eskimos of the Arctic, there is neither timber nor stone but they do have unlimited snow. From this they hew building blocks which are arranged in a rough spiral.

shaped 'key-stone' of snow and drops it in place. Finally he cuts a window facing west and with the piece of snow block which he has removed makes a reflector which sends the last glancing rays of the setting sun into the igloo, through a window cut from clear ice. A temporary overnight igloo may be built in an hour to provide shelter from the cold of the Arctic night, but a more permanent structure may be much larger in capacity. The inside will be hung with skins to provide an insulating inner wall which traps a layer of air between hide and snow and keeps the occupants warm.

Eskimos are hunters and hunters need to evolve kinds of shelter which may be speedily built from the materials available *en route* or constructed of light materials capable of being carried, erected and dismantled with ease. Though the North American Indian, also a hunter, was tech-

nologically limited by his failure to discover the wheel, he devised many forms of vernacular structure. Plains Indians, such as the Blackfeet, used the tipi, a bison skin tent on poles which could be trailed from horseback over long distances and be swiftly erected.

The tent's potential

Many other peoples have devised tents, and a tent culture which extends from the western shores of Africa to the steppes of Mongolia may be traced. Those of the Berber in North Africa are of the 'black tent' kind, made in long bands of goat-and-camel-hair fabric woven on ground looms. The strips are sewn together and reinforced with lengths of decorative webbing which takes the strain of the goat-hair guy ropes. Though their natural dark colour would seem inappropriate to the heat of the desert, their very open weave keeps them well ventilated and cool inside. When sudden rainstorms occur, the fibres contract rapidly to provide a weather-proof shield, while their low contours are a defence against sand-storms and wind.

49

1

1 Many peoples from Africa to Mongolia, such as these Moroccan nomads, have used the tent for centuries. Proof against wind and storm, it can be quickly dismantled and easily carried.

2 A parallel to modern reinforced concrete construction can be found in the wattle and daub method which has been used for building this hut in Uganda.

2

Further east, beyond the Caspian Sea in Turkestan, the black tents give way to the *yurt* of the Kazak, a portable structure which is resilient and proof against storms and wind. It is made of a trellis of sticks, loosely jointed at the intersections, which may be opened out to form a circular wall. Above the trellis wall, lengths of willow are fixed and socketed into a wooden hoop at the crest, the whole structure being covered with mats of felt and held down by horsehair ropes. To the architect today, the advantages of the tent are now being realized. With Frei Otto in the lead, the designers of the new tents are looking again at the methods of making demountable homes invented by the tribesmen of many countries.

The nomad's tent demonstrates a structural principle which is only now becoming the subject of study and experiment in formal architecture; similarly other kinds of vernacular architecture demonstrate further principles of shelter and construction. Poured concrete mass walling has its parallel in the mass walling of poured and dried mud; brick and block constructions have their parallels in adobe

3

construction by which houses are built with sun-dried bricks made of mud and straw; reinforced concrete is paralleled in wattle and daub, a method in which mud is plastered on a wattle-work frame. But there are more subtle principles demonstrated in the use of tension structures, where saplings and thin branches set in the ground and bent until they meet to form a pointed arch employ the tensile strength of the material itself.

Many of the same materials are traditionally employed by communities in widely diverse regions. There are parallels in Chinese roof construction and that of the early wooden houses of Finland, or in the log houses of Michoacan in Mexico and those of Swiss farmhouses. Such comparisons show that similar resources may lead to a similar technology. In regions with heavy timber, people build by laying logs one above another and crossing them

3 In heavily timbered regions like Switzerland, houses are built by laying logs one above the other and crossing them at the corners. A strong roof copes with heavy snowloads.

4 Simple Indian hoggans in Arizona demonstrate how similar resources may lead to similar building techniques, for the wall construction is almost identical to that of a Swiss chalet.

4

at the corners with notched, morticed or pegged methods of jointing. But where one form of roof may be built to resist a periodic snow load, another may need devices to allow the passage of cool air in cross-ventilation.

Simple comparisons of similar technologies may lead, therefore, to oversimplification; often there are many other factors which may determine the nature of a structure or the way it is used. When a natural material is available in abun-

A peasant house from the mountains of Peru has walls of bamboo to allow air to circulate freely, whilst a veranda offers additional shelter from the sun's rays.

dance and has sufficient properties of weight, strength, resilience or portability it may be used; but often the problems of using a material for building may only be overcome with ingenuity. Stone was readily available in ancient Egypt but Egyptian stone columns imitated an earlier technology using materials with very different properties. Here bundles of reeds were tied together to make a sufficiently strong building component where the individual fibres have little or no structural applications; such a technique may still be seen in Syria today.

Makeshift materials

At times a community, through lack of resources of a particular kind, may have to make do with available materials which do not meet all their requirements. In northern Ghana the Fra-Fra tribesmen have evolved structures of circular mud huts with roofs of mud, laid over the elephant grass which grows in abundance during part of the year. But the heavy precipitation in the rainy season invariably damages the roof, causing much discomfort for the occupants of the houses. There is timber in small measure which could be used to reinforce the roofs and provide a more permanent cover, but the trees are far more highly valued for the shade they provide in the merciless heat of a near-equatorial sun. Similarly, in the Spiti province of south-western Tibet, many of the roofs of the mud-constructed buildings are thatched and offer little resistance to the immense falls of snow. There is no stone and not enough timber available; the inhabitants have become accustomed instead to raking off the snow with each fall.

There are, then, practical problems with some indigenous forms which could be solved with the aid of new materials and appropriate technology. But many vernacular structures have met all the requirements of the communities which they

On the swampy mangrove-infested western shores of Malaya where houses push out to sea on narrow stilts the natives have finely adapted their architecture to the conditions.

house and have been refined to an aesthetic. Such is the case with the Dogon, a tribe that lives in a bend of the Niger River in Mali, south of Timbuktu. Their houses cling to the cliff-debris of a high escarpment in a rocky, arid land and are subject to a scorching climate. As the writings of the French anthropologist Marcel Griaule have shown, the Dogon have a highly developed culture in which religion, dance, music, art and social patterns are totally integrated. This is expressed in their mud houses, which seem to grow out of the landscape. Assuming primary forms of cubes and cylinders capped with conical thatch roofs, they have a plastic harmony which is the envy of architects seeking formal unity in their own work. But Griaule has also shown that the positions of living rooms, courtyards, outhouses, walls, even granaries and cooking pots, all have a deep symbolic significance for the Dogon, giving an added dimension to the inner meaning of their buildings which, in our own society, only survives in the most vestigial forms in the new churches and political buildings.

Ill-advised building schemes

Few architects might choose to interfere with such closely knit communities in which buildings and social patterns are so intimately related, and yet the record of new developments and housing schemes in Iraq or Tanzania, northern India or New Mexico, is by no means reassuring.

A tall Fijian house, based on a timber framework, with the characteristic steeply sloping roof; the gap between the thatched walls and the roof allows for ventilation.

Tribal communities have been divided and housed in buildings which have no regard for materials, climate or social structure:

English suburban houses stand in the blazing heat of the desert surrounded by pitiful, infertile 'gardens', while nearby, the *souks* and courtyard houses which they are intended to replace keep cool and comfortable. Such ill-advised building has often occurred in the developing countries where the assimilation of Western technology has also led to the adoption of Western architectural styles. The lessons of the vernacular forms are overlooked, and so too are the resources of energy and creativity which built them.

To a small extent this situation is now being remedied. The policies of destroying the squatter settlements outside certain South American cities have been replaced in some districts by more enlightened ones which assist the homeless in building their own houses in the *barriadas*. Their concerted efforts are providing new vernacular forms.

Not only does vernacular architecture teach us much about the relation of the buildings to the total environment and to the needs of the people which they house; it also indicates a solution to the present and future problems that face us in accommodating the world's rapidly expanding population.

Architecture made new

Shell shapes, tent shapes, roofs with ribs, roofs without, forms are freer
than ever before, thanks to the scope of the new materials and the skill
of those designers who exploit them.

IF 50 PEOPLE were to start with flat sheets of material which could stretch, fold or bend, and were asked to model it to any shape they wanted, the results would be many and varied. In a similar fashion, reinforced concrete has this freedom. Concrete is a material formed by a mixture of cement, sand and small stones whose size depends on the required shape. When water is added to this mixture the material which results can be poured into a mould, or formwork, and formed to any shape.

Concrete is extremely strong when it is compressed under a load but weak when it is pulled apart. However, when steel bars are added in certain positions the new material, known as reinforced concrete, is extremely strong and can be used to cover very large spaces with a minimum of thickness. Certain shapes use less material, now that engineers have discovered the methods of calculating the relative amounts of steel and concrete to be used.

Experiments with folding thick paper will show how a material can be made more rigid along the edge (diagram 1). This is the same principle with which engineers and architects have developed shapes for roof structures. When material

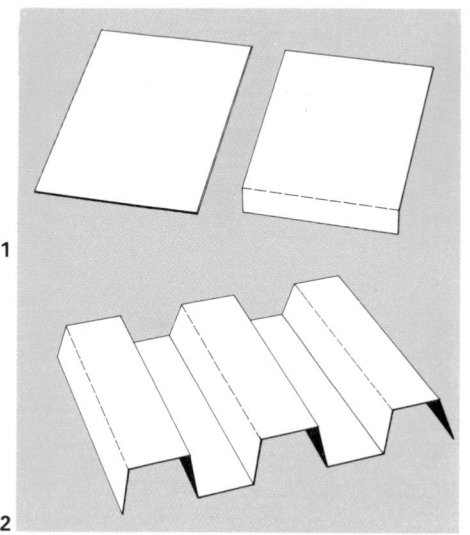

1

2

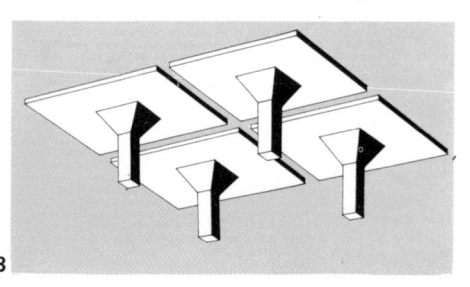

3

is continuously folded, the whole surface becomes more rigid (diagram 2).

One of the first developments was to consider the column and floor as a single unit instead of separate parts (diagram 3). These were called 'mushroom' slab constructions after their similarity to mushrooms, and were used for the first time in high buildings by Robert Maillart, a Swiss structural engineer, in about 1910. With this type of building construction there are no beams and so the internal spaces under the roof can be more freely organized.

These large-scale structures developed further with the transformation of the elongated arch or tunnel vault. The vault had been used by the Romans to build roofs over their public baths, but in their case was generally semi-circular in shape. As engineers realized the shape could be built in reinforced concrete, and the forces could be calculated, it was also recognized that a *catenary* curve – the kind of curve you get if you dangle a chain from both hands held close together – when inverted gives a form of structure that is very strong in tension. This meant that they could make the structure much thinner,

and use very little steel to reinforce it.

Since designers knew that this type of structure would buckle rather than break at any particular point, the vaults were ribbed to prevent such an occurrence. This is shown in the airship hangars at Orly, which were designed by Eugène Freysinnet, a French engineer, and built between 1916 and 1924 (picture 4). The rib in this case was formed by folding the curvature along the horizontal surface to achieve strength at the weakest points. The hangars were 984 feet long and 205 feet high.

Curving round corners

The strength of these arched forms was first understood as rail bridges were being constructed in Europe. Maillart and Freysinnet both began to experience the special qualities of concrete and how it can best be used with a minimum of steelwork and formwork. (Maillart's Arve bridge is shown in picture 5.) Repetitive forms allowed the builders to use the formwork many times over, but it was difficult to provide formwork for the parabolic or catenary arched forms and these types of structure were only used for special buildings such as airship hangars or exhibition stands.

4

Pier Luigi Nervi, an Italian engineer built an aircraft hangar in 1935 where the ribs progress in two directions, a design which allowed him to reduce even further the amount of material required and gave added strength. One disadvantage, however, was that the design for the formwork became more complex.

Structure had previously been conceived in terms of two dimensions which were repeated down the length of the building, as we can see in the airship hangars at Orly. But the bridges that curved round corners, and the curved corners of sports stadia made engineers realize that such structures are three-dimensional. And with this realization the ribbed structures by Nervi came into their own.

He used these ribbed structures over many large spaces, including the Sports Palace for the 1960 Olympic Games in Rome, and exhibition halls. In the Sports Palace the ribs are exposed outside the edge of the building and the top surface gently rests over the ribs (pictures 6 and 7).

A further development occurred when several engineers realized that if the roof was not too wide it was possible to eliminate the ribs, provided the roof still maintained its catenary curved shape. Several roofs were built up to 100 feet in length, and perhaps 20 or 30 feet wide, but not wide enough to allow buckling. These roofs were called 'shell' structures for their similarity in curvature and thickness to beach shells. These individual shell roofs were often spaced apart to allow windows to be placed between them. Their

7

repetitive nature allowed easy fabrication because the formwork could be used several times.

These 'shell' roofs were used extensively by an architect called Felix Candela who was born in Spain in 1910 and went to Mexico in 1939. He built his first shell catenary roof in 1949. The first shell roofs, like the airship hangar at Orly, only curved in a single direction. Then architects realized that curvature in more than one direction could be achieved in order to obtain greater strength with less material; compound curvature roofs were developed, predominantly by Felix Candela (diagram 8).

One of the problems with double curvature is that the formwork tends to become very difficult to erect to the required shape. This has meant that such roofs have developed to a greater degree in countries where there are ample supplies of timber

and cheap labour.

Nevertheless, it was understood that one or two double curvature shapes could be formed with a series of straight wires slightly twisted along their lengths (pictures 9 and 10). The tall cooling towers of nuclear power stations are double curvature shapes and can be constructed in a similar manner using a formwork of straight boarding.

These hyperbolic-paraboloid shapes are known as *hypar* shells and continue to be used in Mexico in many forms. They rarely exceed two inches in thickness and are often as thin as a half-inch.

One of the most interesting hypar roofs by Felix Candela is the roof of the Cosmic Ray Laboratory at Mexico City University (picture 11). The roof had to be thin enough to admit cosmic rays, and was constructed to a total thickness of five-eighths of an inch. At the top of the roof,

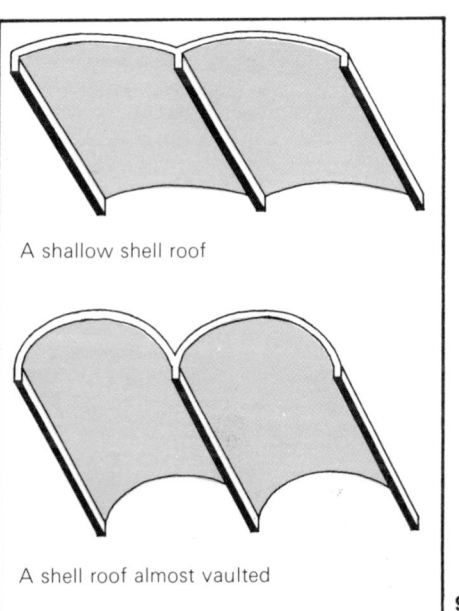

A shallow shell roof

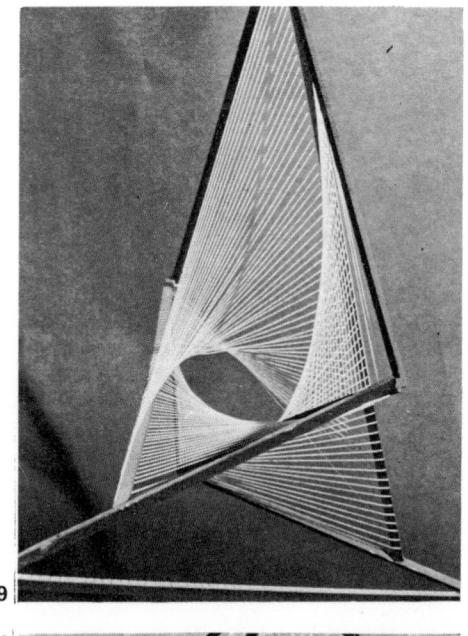

A shell roof almost vaulted

A shell roof composed of double curvature

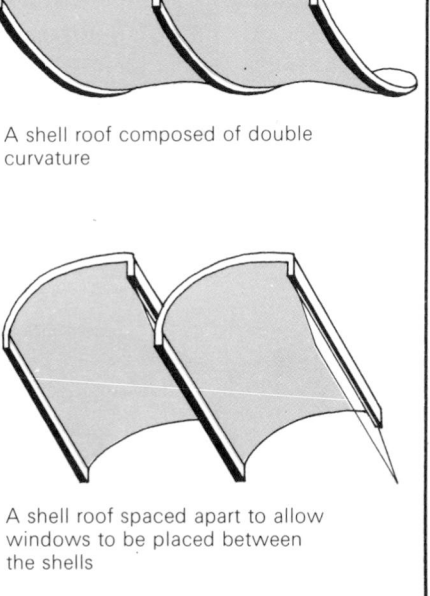

A shell roof spaced apart to allow windows to be placed between the shells

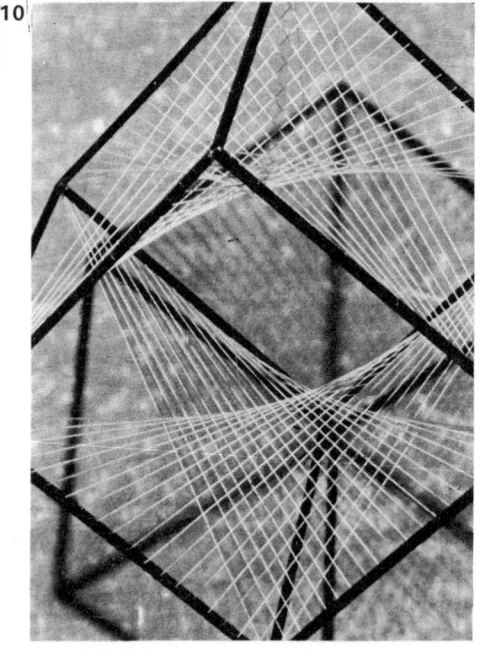

1

turned to other methods of construction. Compound folding is now frequently found, since the formwork can be used again and again. These structures are similar to those achieved by folding paper in more than one direction (pictures 14 and 15).

Experiments with paper have given many designers ideas for roof and wall shapes, the folds becoming equivalent to a complex arrangement of beams which make the whole structure very rigid. Some of these folded structures are now being made in plastics. The introduction of this versatile material encouraged architects and engineers to develop even thinner structures to the point where the surface is almost literally a membrane or skin.

Frei Otto, a German architect who designed the West German stand at Expo '67 in Montreal used a type of glass-reinforced plastic which was formed to the

each square foot of the total thickness only weighs about eight pounds. The roof contained a small amount of steel wire, which was theoretically unnecessary, but was put there to offset stresses imposed upon the building by earthquakes and high winds. All of his roof structures have been truly functional and the shape of the roof always expresses the full performance of the reinforced concrete rather than just emphasizing the form itself.

Other architects, however, have equally successfully utilized the material qualities of the concrete to express exciting forms. Oscar Niemeyer, a Brazilian architect, designed several buildings in the new city of Brazilia. The illustration (picture 12) shows part of the President's Palace and indicates how the shape is not necessarily just functional but expresses the beauty and strength of form. The private chapel of the President's Palace (picture 13) shows how a double curvature in reinforced concrete has been used for the walls instead of for the roof structure, the roof being hidden behind the walls.

Compound curvature is one facet of the development of large-scale structures, but it has become very expensive to erect in Europe. And so architects and engineers

13

14

15

same shape as a tent. It used steel guy ropes to maintain it in position, and metal struts like tent posts where necessary. In the same way as the catenary curve gives the curvature for a shell roof, the tent structure for the West German pavilion was given its shape by first designing it in model form in an upside-down position to allow the shape, in this case a three-dimensional one, to fall to its natural position. After modification the most satisfactory shape was resolved.

A further advantage of these membrane or tent structures is that the plastic can be translucent, since the reinforcement is now glassfibre and not steel. A translucent resin replaces the concrete, thus allowing light to penetrate the roof itself; there is consequently no necessity to insert windows or rooflights in the roof and thus reduce the strength.

It seems to the casual observer almost incredible that roofs so strong and yet so thin could exist without breaking. This is nevertheless the case and it has only been possible because creative men have worked hard to understand the characteristics of their materials. They have developed new ideas for bigger and more economic roofs, geometrically extremely complex, which retain elegant shapes and are exciting for people to look at.

Index

'p' after a page number means there is a relevant illustration on that page
'c' after a page number means there is relevant material in a caption on that page